Against All Odds

Vol 1: The Black Box Report

ISBN: 979-8-9938017-0-4

Cover design: Daniel Giavelli

www.AgainstAllOddsSeries.com

For God, the author of every system, the Architect of every mercy. And for my family, who endured the wreckage while I learned what grace meant.

Statement of Intent

I am an instrument in the hands of God. The words that follow are not written from ambition, pride, or rebellion but from obedience. I did not choose this path, I was built for it. My entire life has been preparation for this moment, every system I designed, every failure I dissected, every silence I endured. Each one was calibration. I have always lived between worlds, the technician and the engineer, the material and the unseen. I was never meant to belong to either side but to stand in the space between them, to translate what one cannot say and the other cannot measure. Against All Odds began from that position. This is only the first record of a larger body of work, a continuing investigation into the patterns that connect all things. Through these pages, I do not preach. I reveal. My purpose is to show that the patterns of creation are not random, that every mechanism echoes its Maker. I speak through the language of systems, because systems cannot lie. Physics, code, machinery, biology, all of them bear the same signature. And if you look closely enough, you will see it too. This work is my bridge, from man to machine, from logic to faith, from design to the Designer. I am not here to claim authorship of truth, only to align with it. My task is to listen, to interpret, and to translate the design as clearly as I can. The intent is not to convince, but to awaken. If you read these words and feel something stir, a question, a spark, a pattern forming where there was once noise, then the work is doing what it was meant to do. Because the truth does not need to be forced. It only needs to be revealed.

Observation logged

Initialization complete

Table Of Contents

Prologue...1

The Morning After.............................. 1

Flashbacks in the Silence.....................5

Engineering Eyes................................7

California..9

The Hook...10

From Fracture to Foundation................ 11

Chapter 1.....................................13

Born Broken....................................13

Street Classroom..............................16

The Line and the Scar........................ 19

The Transfer.................................... 22

Running on Empty............................. 25

Run away.. 28

The Cycle Tightens............................ 30

Fault Line..32

Shockwave...................................... 34

Chapter 2..................................... 37

Circuits of Control............................ 37

Fuel and Fire................................... 40

Load Bearing................................... 43

The Catalyst.................................... 46

Engines of Fire................................. 48

Chapter 3... **53**

Resonant Flow...53

The Few Who Stayed..................................55

Condensed Time..57

Cracks in the Armor....................................59

The Illusion of Control................................60

Chapter 4... **63**

Pressure Test..63

System Degradation...................................65

Critical Load...67

Failure Event..69

Chapter 5... **72**

Telemetry Review.......................................72

The Filter...74

Boundaries of Love....................................76

Hidden Code of Reality...............................78

Chapter 6... **81**

The Law of Decay......................................81

Resistance and Calibration.........................83

Grounded Current.....................................85

Chapter 7... **89**

Observer and Observed..............................89

Faith as Measurement...............................93

Hidden Observer......................................95

Chapter 8...**98**

Destructive Interference.............................98

Harmonic Alignment................................100

The Frequency of Grace............................102

Synthetic Resonance................................105

Chapter 9..107

   Fractals of Life... 107

   The Golden Ratio... 110

   Nonlinear Redemption...................................112

Chapter 10... 115

   NPC Loops... 115

   Branching Paths.. 117

   Breaking the Loop.. 119

Chapter 11..123

   Temptation as Test....................................... 123

   Signal Integrity...125

   Emotional Frequencies..................................128

   Error Correction.. 129

Chapter 12... 133

   Closed Loop Faith.. 133

   Redundancy and Mercy................................. 135

   Adaptive Control... 137

Chapter 13... 141

   Reading the Black Box.................................. 141

   Feedback Equilibrium.................................. 143

   Law of Reference Frame................................144

   Grace as Calibration....................................145

   Signal Flare.. 149

Epilogue... 153

   The Black Box Report................................... 153

   Final Transmission....................................... 156

About the Author..159

Prologue

The Fracture

When the system breaks, data becomes prayer

The Morning After

I woke up on a July 2025 morning in South Texas feeling like death had crawled into my bed and left me behind. My mouth tasted metallic, the stale liquor still ghosting my tongue. My skin was clammy and cold though I was sweating. My head throbbed like steel under a hammer. My stomach was hollow but twisted with nausea. I gagged over the toilet and produced nothing, just dry heaves that racked my ribs and throat. When I lifted my head, the morning light hit the bathroom tile just right. It scattered through the water pooled near my hand, breaking into color. For a second, I just stared. It was the first quiet spark after the blackout, proof that something still moved, that life hadn't shut off completely. Outside, a bird called once, sharp and clear, and the sound cut through the hangover haze like a small mercy. The world was still running its system. I was still part of it. The air smelled faintly of wood splinters and gasoline. Somewhere outside, the sharp tang of rubber hung in the heat, a reminder of what my truck had endured. For a long moment I didn't know where I was. The blinds were drawn, thin slats of light cutting through onto the wreckage of another night. Everything looked slightly unfamiliar, as if I had wandered into a stranger's life that happened to have my name on it. I staggered to the mirror. The face looking back wasn't mine. Pale. Sunken. Eyes red and bloodshot. Lips cracked. He looked like a man half-buried. I gripped the counter, fighting dizziness, and the first thought carved its way through the fog. "What the fuck did I just do again?" The house answered for me. The front door splintered, a bookshelf shattered, holes punched into drywall, bedroom doors cracked off their hinges. Out in the yard, the wreckage continued. My son's slip-n-slide shredded, the patio umbrella snapped like a twig. My truck bore scars too. The rims were bent, tires flat-spotted from locking up, still somehow holding air. Every broken thing was a breadcrumb pointing back to me.

Telemetry Insert

Fault Tree Initiation

Inputs: *System breach confirmed and visual logging initiated.*

State: *Operator transitions from reaction to analysis.*

Output: *Observation stabilizes emotional load. Data capture begins.*

This wasn't new. I had blacked out hundreds of times before. But this time was different. My son had stepped in. That's what my wife told me when she finally emerged later that morning. She had spent the night barricaded in my youngest son's room, while both of my kids slept together, apart from the chaos. Her face was pale, not with surprise but exhaustion. Her voice was flat, recounting how violent I had become, how I had nearly choked her unconscious in a headlock, and how I had gotten violent toward our oldest son and he had to take things into his own hands to stop me. And then she told me about the sheriff. The same man who had been to my house before. He saw the holes, the broken furniture, the wrecked yard. He knew the pattern. But instead of dragging me off in cuffs that night, he spoke to me like a human being. He showed me mercy I hadn't earned. That hit harder than any hangover. Undeserved grace, a mirror I couldn't look away from. I didn't feel saved. I didn't feel forgiven. I felt exposed. The truth was brutal. I had been running on poison. Barely eating, barely sleeping except for drunken pass-outs. My body was collapsing. My mind unraveling. The only thing I wanted was to disappear. I hated myself. I wanted to die. But I wasn't dead. Somehow, after years of drinking, after wrecked cars and wrecked nights, after chaos that should have destroyed me, I was still alive. Still breathing. Still here. And that fact was unbearable. Why me? Why again? Why was I spared when all I left behind was wreckage? If chaos was all there was, I should have been gone. But I wasn't. That meant something else was at work. I didn't know what to call it yet. But I knew one thing with clarity, I couldn't keep the addiction cycle going. The structure had failed. I had to leave and rebuild. So I called my brother in California. My voice cracked as I asked him to come get me, to take me away from the ruins I had made of my life. That call didn't fix anything. It didn't erase the shame or the damage. But it was a signal flare from the pit. The light caught a shallow puddle by the porch and split into color like a small prism hiding in mud. Far off, a plane lifted from the airport and drew a thin sound across the morning. Birds started up in the trees with that calm insistence they have after a storm. Everything kept moving. Time kept its rhythm. The house still smelled like the night before and my body carried the aches to prove it, but my chest was rising and falling on its own. Heart steady. Thoughts a little clearer than they had any right to be. I wanted the world to pause and look at me, to mark what had just happened, but it did not. It just ticked forward. That quiet indifference felt like mercy. Life was still here, waiting for me to notice it. I stood there longer than I needed to, listening to the plane fade and the birds hold their line, and let the simple fact land. I was alive. The system still ran.

Flashbacks in the Silence

As I waited, memories surfaced uninvited, like fragments of a film spooling backward. Each one was a frame of entropy, small but connected, a thumbprint of the chaos I'd been carrying long before that July morning. I remembered growing up in Moreno Valley, a kid in the 1990s ghetto, a minority surrounded by gangs and violence. Crime scene tape was as common as chain-link fences. "Ghetto birds" or the neighborhood Police helicopters, hovered like insects in the night, their searchlights crawling across rooftops and faces. Drive-bys cracked the silence open like thunder. Sirens were background music, the city breathing chaos through a loudspeaker. You learned early what not to wear, where not to walk, and how long to hold someone's gaze. Respect wasn't earned with kindness, it was enforced with fear. When we moved to Costa Mesa at around eleven years old, I thought it would change everything. Cleaner streets. Less noise. Different zip code. But the fracture came with me, invisible but intact, a hairline crack running through glass. Moreno Valley had been raw chaos and survival through instinct. Costa Mesa was a different kind of trap, rules, tickets, authority. By twelve, I was getting stopped constantly. Tickets for riding my bike without a helmet. Tickets for smoking cigarettes. Tickets for jaywalking. The same reflexes that kept me alive in the ghetto now made me a target in the suburbs. The violence had changed shape and it wore badges instead of colors. I remembered being twelve, already wandering into Satanism, a boy too young to vote but old enough to light black candles and recite rituals I barely understood. It had started as curiosity, a way to feel powerful in a world where I felt powerless. But when I whispered those invocations, the air seemed to shift. My room felt colder. Shadows thicker. I had opened doors I couldn't close. Within months, more entropy rushed into my life slowly. It showed in subtle ways, but quickly I noticed friends dying of cancer, accidents, drug overdoses, others arrested. Chaos multiplying around me with mechanical precision. It felt like a filter was running, stripping away innocence and exposing something darker in all of us. I remembered my father. Not really a father at all, just a man I'd seen a handful of times, always smelling of alcohol, his eyes dulled by something I didn't yet have a name for. An addict. A drifter. A ghost with my DNA but not my care. I had promised myself I'd never become him. And yet here I was, worse in some ways, my chaos more efficient, my destruction more calculated. At thirteen, I was arrested. At that age, you're supposed to be learning multiplication tables, not Miranda rights. Different streets, same entropy. The system was the same game, just dressed in cleaner clothes. And I was still watching, taking notes, learning the new rules of a different kind of chaos. And I remembered the nights of drinking that escalated after 2020. At first it was a release, then a habit, then a second skin. Blackouts became normal. Violence, too. Cars wrecked. Arguments turned into holes in drywall. The house itself became a map of my failures, each broken door its own drunken story, each splinter of wood a data point I didn't want to read.

Engineering Eyes

At SpaceX I had learned something early, Chaos always leaves a signature. It doesn't matter how complex the system is, engines, software, plumbing, people, if you know what you're looking for, the truth is in the data. Every explosion leaves a fingerprint. Every anomaly hums at its own frequency. Strain gauges don't lie. Pressure sensors don't lie. They tell the story no one wants to read. Where stress built up, where design cracked, where the system was already failing long before the moment of failure. That morning in South Texas, as I walked through the wreckage of my home, my eyes flicked from damage to damage the way they used to flick from screen to screen in the control room. Bent rims weren't just bent rims, they were pressure spikes, uncommanded thrust. Broken doors weren't just broken doors, they were redline alarms, systems pushed past limits. Splintered furniture, holes in drywall, a wife barricaded with a child, those weren't random outcomes. They were telemetry of a life spinning out of control. My family sleeping apart from me wasn't just a sad detail. It was the ultimate abort call, the clearest warning in the system. In rockets, when an alarm goes off, you have seconds to respond. Ignore it, and you don't just lose the test article, you lose months of work, millions of dollars, sometimes lives. The countdown doesn't stop because you're tired or distracted. The physics don't care about your feelings. Reality is hardcoded. In life, you can ignore alarms longer. You can drink over them, rationalize them, pretend they're false positives. You can live months, years, decades with warning lights flashing on every panel. But the end is the same. Systems fail. Structures collapse. People break. That morning I understood it in a way I never had before. My life wasn't random chaos. It was a system under load, bleeding data, screaming warnings. And like a rocket test, it had reached the point where either you abort or you explode. Psychologists call it the addiction cycle. Engineers call it structural fatigue. Both end the same way if ignored. Collapse. Systems that ignore redlines only last until their next test cycle. Mine was coming fast.

Telemetry Insert

Systems Thinking Online

Inputs: *Impact event, household silence, disorientation*

State: *Perception switches from story to signal*

Output: *Pattern recognition engaged, blame paused*

California

When my brother pulled up, it was in a rental car. That somehow made the moment sharper. Temporary. Like everything in my life was on loan, patched together just long enough to get me moving again. Before I could leave, I had to fix a few things. The house was broken in ways I couldn't ignore. If it wasn't already pouring out chaos, my water heater decided that morning was the day to give out, adding one more failure to the list. I stood there, hungover and hollow, wrestling with pipes and fittings, repairing the front door I had splintered with my own hands. It was surreal, patching the very wounds I had inflicted, as if I couldn't escape until I acknowledged them one last time. When the door finally closed again on its hinges and the water heater rumbled back to life, I dropped my tools, grabbed my bag, and walked out. My brother waited patiently, engine running. I slid into the rental's passenger seat and didn't look back. The drive west felt like an extraction. South Texas faded in the rearview, the mesquite trees, the canal by my property, the scars of a battlefield I had made with my own hands. Every mile was a burn sequence, a stage separation. Chaos fell away behind me like a discarded booster. Ahead was the silence of space. I wasn't going to California to find God. I already had two years earlier, after spending almost twenty years trying to disprove His existence. Now I had been living gratefully for Him ever since, but I was still human and made mistakes. California was something different. It was survival. It was the quiet after the explosion, the vacuum where fragments could finally settle. The place where I could breathe long enough to ask what my life meant. And it was in that silence that I decided to write this book. Not as a confession. Not as a self-help manual. But as a black box report of a crash that should have ended me, and didn't.

The Hook

This book didn't begin as a testimony. It began as a rebellion. For eighteen years I tried to disprove God, not casually but methodically. I treated faith like an engineering problem. I took every paradox, every contradiction, every mystery I could find, physics, psychology, history, philosophy, and put it on the bench, tested it, stressed it, tried to break it. I built a map of the universe without Him. I wanted a model that didn't need a Creator, a theory of everything where meaning was an accident. But the deeper I went, the more I kept finding fingerprints. Patterns. Design. A thumbprint of order hidden inside the chaos. And when I stepped back, I realized something that hit me harder than any textbook. My own life mirrored the universe I was trying to chart. It wasn't random. It was chaotic, yes, but not meaningless. Entropy, but also calibration. Destruction, but also survival. That July morning in South Texas was my singularity, the point where my old self collapsed in on itself. A lifetime of running, doubting, and self-inflicted entropy compressed into one violent night and one unbearable morning. I wasn't dead. Somehow I was still alive. And that meant the testing phase was over. It was time to start telling the truth, not a clean story, not a heroic arc, but the real telemetry of a crash that should have ended me. This book is that black box report. The flight data of a life I tried to fly without a pilot. The signal flare from the pit. And maybe, in my chaos, trauma cycles, and desperation, you'll recognize your own. If you're allergic to sermons, good. So am I. This isn't a conversion tract, it's a field report. If you bring zero faith and a high BS meter, you're my target reader, because what follows is patterns you can test, not vibes you have to feel. No hero edits, no mystical fog. If a claim can't be mapped to cause and effect in real life, it doesn't stay in this book. What you'll get in these pages:

Lived scenes → Testable principles → Simple protocols

From Fracture to Foundation

Leaving Texas behind didn't erase the wreckage, it just gave me silence long enough to hear it echo. California wasn't redemption, it was a reset button, a pause between the collapse and whatever came next. I wasn't chasing religion when I got there. I had already become a believer two years earlier, after nearly two decades of trying to prove the opposite. That part of the story mattered, but it wasn't the beginning. The fracture that morning in Texas wasn't caused by God or healed by God alone. It was the culmination of something older, something baked into me from birth. If I wanted to understand why my life kept cycling back to chaos, I had to trace it back to the foundation, the cracks that were already there before I ever took a drink, before I ever pulled a knife, before I ever blacked out. That's where this story really begins.

Anchor Card

Law of First Readout: *Chaos becomes data*

Principle: *Chaos reveals design when viewed through data, not denial.*

Protocol: *Observe, record, recalibrate.*

Proof: *The wreckage became my first system readout, not my tomb.*

Observation logged

Chapter 1

Foundations Cracked from the Start

The Architecture of Pain and Survival

Born Broken

I wasn't supposed to be here. I was born dead, six minutes without a pulse. A prolapsed cord strangled my entry into the world, and when they pulled me out in an emergency C section, I was lifeless. Doctors shocked my chest, pumped tiny compressions, breathed air into lungs that refused to move. Finally I gasped. A heartbeat. A body animated again. From the beginning, my life was a glitch in the system, survival against odds that said otherwise. I was told that when I was barely old enough to walk, I took apart a pedal go-kart just to see what was inside. Nobody taught me. I didn't know the words for chain or gear or torque, but I wanted to see what made the wheels move. I remember staring at the parts scattered across the driveway, sunlight glinting off the small bolts as if the pieces were alive. Later, around three or four, I'd sit beside my bike and spin the pedals by hand, studying how every link of the chain slid into place. Even the door latches on cars fascinated me, the way a click and a spring could decide whether something was safe or open. I wasn't breaking things. I was learning how motion became control. Before I ever had language for systems, I already needed to know how they worked. That was my first form of faith. Believing that if I understood the mechanism, I might survive the chaos around it. My mother already carried fractures of her own. She had five kids from a previous marriage, went through a messy divorce, and then met my biological father, her brother's friend, on a camping trip. I was the result. He was never a father. More like a donor. He was an alcoholic, a drifter, in and out of chaos, and my mom eventually threw him out when I was two. I have no memory of him being there, just stories of drunken destruction and a ghost who left a wound. By the time I was old enough to take in the world, my mom was working long days, trying to hold together the pieces of her life. That meant I was left with babysitters, and often with the streets. We lived in a ghetto apartment complex in Moreno Valley. I was three, maybe four, when I started wandering out of the apartment while the babysitter slept. Outside was another kind of classroom. Crime scene tape went up and down like the seasons. Gangs circled the courtyards, drive-bys cracked the silence, police helicopters, the ghetto bird, hummed above almost nightly. Shootouts were not rare. Prostitution, drug deals, people passed out in the fields. A constant theater of survival and destruction. The kids around me mirrored the adults. We played cops and robbers, but everyone wanted to be the robber. We imitated drunks staggering, slurred speech, collapsing into laughter. Play fighting always had an edge of real violence. Innocence was acting out the toxicity we saw every day. But I did not join in fully. I was always on the outside, watching. Even as a minority in that environment, I did not care what people thought of me. I had this instinct that I was there to observe, not belong. I saw patterns others did not. I noticed how anger escalated, how respect worked, how chaos followed certain rhythms. If I stepped in, it was only to correct something directly in front of me. Mostly I just stood back. Watching. Learning. It is strange to say, but even then I felt like a main character in a world full of NPCs. Most people moved in loops, acting out scripts written by poverty, addiction, and violence. I felt pulled out of the game somehow, like I was supposed to understand it rather than be consumed by it. That distance was my survival. Yet survival was fragile. One word, one mistake, could turn the crowd against me. When I was eight, I found out how thin that line was. I had always been more curious than cautious, always asking questions out loud. One day I heard older kids in the neighborhood calling each other the N word. I did not know what it meant. I asked straight out why they used it and what it was supposed to mean. Before anyone could answer, one of the kids lunged at me, threw me in a chokehold against a driveway, rage written on his face. To him I had not asked a question, I had crossed a line. Later some of the older guys explained it to me, told me about slavery, told me why it was a word with weight. But the moment had already passed. What could have been a teaching opportunity turned into violence. That was the environment. Most people did not have the patience or perspective to see intent before reacting. Everything was reflex, survival, reaction. I walked away with a scar that was not physical but mental. I realized people judge by covers, not contents. Misunderstanding can escalate faster than facts can catch up. Sometimes anger kills a conversation before it can bloom into understanding. And I realized I wanted no part of that cycle. I saw how kids absorbed their parents' toxicity like sponges. Innocence was corrupted by imitation, adults blind to how their actions rippled outward into their children. It was like watching a loop you already knew the ending to. Play acting drunk becomes drinking for real. Play fighting becomes actual violence. Pretending to be robbers becomes the first real theft. By twelve I had lived long enough in that environment to act swiftly to threats. If someone said something to you, you had to take it as real and deal with it on the spot. There was no ignoring it. Hesitation was weakness.

Street Classroom

Moreno Valley was not a neighborhood, it was a system under constant vibration. You could feel the tension in the air, the hum of violence like static before lightning. It was the 1990s and the city pulsed with gang colors, police sirens, and heat that never really cooled. Crime scene tape fluttered like flags in the wind. The ghetto birds, the police helicopters, hovered at night, their searchlights crawling across rooftops and backyards. You learned to keep your eyes open, not because you were scared but because looking away could get you hurt. School was not where I learned about survival. The streets were. Moreno Valley was divided by invisible borders. One wrong street, one wrong glance, one wrong shirt color, and you could find yourself surrounded. Kids my age carried trauma like homework. Some had guns. Some had nothing but fear. All of us understood that power came from attention, where you looked, how long, and what you let people see. That is where my education really began. I started watching. Not just the fights or the cops or the chaos, but patterns. The rhythm of cause and effect. I noticed that people who reacted fast got trapped faster. Anger made you predictable. Pride made you visible. Silence made you invisible. You could disappear in plain sight if you paid attention. That instinct to observe rather than react became my first survival system. I did not know it then, but I was living the observer effect. The act of observation changes the system being observed. By watching carefully I could alter my outcomes. I could see danger forming before it reached me. I could sense when a situation was about to turn. It was not about being smart. It was about being tuned. Entropy was everywhere around me, but I learned to read it like weather. When tension built on the block it was like pressure in a system. Unreleased, it would explode. Violence was not random. It was data. Someone disrespected someone's cousin, someone got jumped, someone grabbed a gun. Every act had a cause. Every cause had a pattern. If I could recognize the pattern early enough, I could get clear before the detonation. It did not make me fearless. It made me efficient. Other kids joined crews for safety. I stayed unaffiliated, which was its own kind of danger. Alone but mobile. I kept my head down and my ears open. I watched how people moved, how they spoke when they were lying, how fear made them twitch. My curiosity, the same one that used to get me in trouble at home, became armor. Sometimes I wondered if I was meant to be that way. Free will or determinism lived in me early even if I did not have the words yet. Did I choose this vigilance, or was it forced on me by chaos. Every night that ended with sirens I thought about it. Maybe everyone was just reacting to the conditions they were born into, heat, poverty, neglect, fear. Maybe choice was an illusion. Even if it was, I learned how to use it. If the system was rigged I would treat it like an experiment. If life was going to break me, I would study how. If you understand the way something breaks, you can understand how to make it stronger next time. Looking back now I realize that Moreno Valley taught me the foundation of my worldview. Nothing fails without a reason. Nothing breaks clean. Everything leaves data. The violence, the chaos, the fear, they were all signals. I was the kid in the corner logging every one of them without knowing those notes would one day become the framework I used to analyze rockets, addiction, and faith itself. In that sense the ghetto was not just survival. It was my first laboratory.

The Line and the Scar

There's a line every kid crosses once, and it's never the same line twice. For some, it's stealing candy from a store. For others, it's the first lie that actually works. For me, it was realizing that doing the right thing didn't mean you'd be treated right. I was twelve the first time I saw that clearly. It happened fast, the way trouble always does. One moment right when I moved to Costa Mesa, I was defending myself, the next I was on the ground, staring up at a crowd that had already made up its mind. Another kid, older and bigger, decided I was his target that day. He shoved me, called me names, tried to humiliate me in front of everyone. I pushed back. That's all it took. Chaos doesn't need reason, it just needs ignition. The next few seconds blurred into fists, adrenaline, and instinct. By the time it was over, I had a bloody lip and a head full of confusion. My heart was pounding, and I was trying to catch my breath. I felt the immediate effects of injury in the form of scrapes and bumps that will soon turn into bruises. Nobody cared who started it. The story was already written before I could speak. The next day I had a pocket knife on me I carried when the teachers pulled me into the office. They didn't ask what happened. They didn't ask why. They just told me I was being expelled for bringing the knife to school and fighting. No questions, no context, just a decision. I sat there trying to explain, but their faces were already made of stone. The letter had already been typed. My mother's face when she picked me up said everything, disappointment layered over exhaustion. Not anger, just that deep hollow sadness parents get when they're too tired to keep pretending it'll be different next time. That day taught me something brutal. In systems, whether mechanical, social, or spiritual, the labels you wear can matter more than the truth you live. Once they stamp you as problematic, every output after that is treated like an error. That was my first scar. Not the kind you see, but one that split something deeper. It was the fracture between justice and experience. I started to understand the duality of the world, that right and wrong didn't live in the same place. Doing what felt honorable could still get you punished. Staying silent could save you, even if it meant swallowing truth. It wasn't fairness I learned that day, it was calibration. That's when I stopped expecting adults to protect me. I stopped expecting the world to make sense. I started expecting entropy. But buried in that moment was something else too, a kind of awakening. If systems can misfire, then so can judgments. If outcomes don't match inputs, then the model is wrong. I didn't have the words for it yet, but that was my first taste of the problem of evil. How order can exist in a world where doing good gets punished. I didn't cry that night. I didn't talk about it. Instead, I got quiet. I built walls. I hardened my edges the way metal does after heat treatment, stronger on the surface but more brittle inside. The anger came later, disguised as pride. But under it, there was grief. That's the thing about early wounds, they don't bleed forever, but they never stop humming. You carry the frequency of that moment inside you, and it colors everything after. Teachers became cops in my mind. Rules became traps. And I became exactly what the system predicted I'd be. Defiant, detached, observant, but always distant. When people looked at me after that, they didn't see a kid. They saw a problem to contain. And part of me started believing them. That's how the expectation paradox works. The moment the world expects your failure, you start to live down to it. It becomes gravity. But every system under pressure eventually finds its load limit, and that moment was mine. The line I crossed that day wasn't just between right and wrong. It was between being seen and being scanned. Between being human and being data. And once that switch flipped, there was no going back. A few months later, something small shifted. I was in class and some kid started clowning on my shoes. Cheap ones from Payless Shoes with the logo peeling off. I didn't have much to say back, I just sat there and took it. Before it could go further, another kid spoke up. "Leave him alone," he said, plain and quiet, like it wasn't even worth the fight. The room went still for a second, and then everyone moved on. I never forgot that moment. He didn't have to do it. He just did. After that we'd nod at each other in passing, a silent acknowledgment that someone had seen me and didn't look away. It was the first time I realized the world still had good circuits. People who carried current when mine was out. Looking back now, I can see how close it all could have gone the other way. One more bad day, one more wrong corner, one more fight that didn't end. Somehow, I made it through. I didn't see it as grace then, but it was. The scar stayed, but so did the breath that followed. It could have been worse. It always could have been worse.

The Transfer

When we left Moreno Valley, I thought we were leaving chaos behind. Costa Mesa sounded like peace, beach air, cleaner streets, no gunshots in the night. I was eleven, still young enough to believe that geography could fix destiny. But the first thing I learned was that chaos doesn't die when you move. It just changes its uniform. In Moreno Valley, chaos had worn gang colors. In Costa Mesa, it wore badges and clipboards. One system ran on violence. The other ran on control. I was used to scanning danger in people, their posture, tone, the way eyes moved before hands did. But here, the threats came as tickets, warnings, detentions. Bureaucracy instead of bullets. The cops didn't chase us for what we did, but for what we were. Kids in the wrong place, at the wrong time, with the wrong faces. At twelve, I started collecting citations like souvenirs. Tickets for riding my bike without a helmet. Tickets for smoking cigarettes. Tickets for jaywalking.

Every piece of paper felt like another reminder that I didn't belong anywhere. It was the same game, just with different rules. Back in the ghetto, you learned how to survive fast. Out here, survival meant learning how to submit. The streets didn't test your strength, they tested your compliance. That shift messed with my wiring. I had spent years teaching my nervous system that hesitation could get you hurt. Now, hesitation was what they wanted, obedience, deference, silence. It was a paradox my brain couldn't reconcile. Free will versus determinism wasn't a philosophy class, it was my life. I could choose, but my choices had already been labeled. Every move I made was predetermined by how I looked, where I lived, and what box I fit into. And yet, even then, I was watching. That outsider instinct hadn't left, it just recalibrated. In Moreno Valley, I observed patterns of violence. In Costa Mesa, I observed patterns of power. Both operated on feedback loops, reward and punishment, fear and control. Both taught the same lesson, systems protect themselves. The observer effect showed up again, though I didn't know its name yet. I realized that once you become aware of how a system sees you, you start to change the way you move inside it. You shift tone, posture, eye contact. You perform the version of yourself least likely to trigger an alarm. It's survival through adaptation, but every adaptation costs a piece of authenticity. I was becoming fluent in both dialects of chaos. I could talk to the streets and the system, and understand both frequencies. But the more fluent I became, the more fractured I felt. Costa Mesa was supposed to be safe, but I felt more trapped than ever. In Moreno Valley, I could spot danger coming. In Costa Mesa, danger smiled and handed me a citation. It was duality made physical, light disguised as order, dark disguised as freedom. At thirteen, it all finally broke. A group of kids and I got caught smoking weed at school and a few of us decided to break into the school a few nights later and vandalize the classroom of the teacher that found us. In Moreno Valley, that moment would've ended with a finger wag and a lesson learned. In Costa Mesa, it ended with expulsion and the courts involved. I remember sitting in the principal's office, my hands clenched, watching fluorescent lights buzz overhead. It felt unreal. The same instinct that had kept me alive for years had just gotten me thrown out. That's when I learned something about systems no one teaches you. They don't care about your context, only your compliance. That moment rewired me. It was the first time I realized that survival instincts have half-lives. What once kept you alive eventually gets you labeled a threat. The tools that protected me in one world condemned me in another. And maybe that's the cruelest part of growing up in chaos. You adapt to survive, but those adaptations become the very things that destroy you when the environment changes. Costa Mesa was supposed to be safety. For me, it was just another kind of cage.

Running on Empty

Shortly after, we moved from Costa Mesa to Huntington beach. Right next to Stacie, who would later become my wife. Probation felt like freedom until I realized it was just a longer leash. At first, I told myself it was a second chance, proof that maybe I could still fix things. But it didn't take long to see it for what it was, another system designed to watch, not guide. Probation officers didn't mentor you. They measured you. They took notes. They waited for you to fail. I was thirteen, then fourteen, running on fumes. Every decision I made was reaction, not direction. There was no father figure. No model for what strength actually looked like, only examples of what not to become. My mom worked nonstop, trying to hold everything together. I could see the exhaustion in her eyes when she looked at me, as if she was staring at a reflection of all the chaos she'd tried to escape. Without realizing it, I'd become both symptom and system. My behavior wasn't random. It was predictable. Root cause analysis 101, you could trace every bad decision back to an earlier fracture. Neglect became insecurity. Insecurity became defiance. Defiance became survival. The cycle was simple, act out, get caught, get punished, promise to do better, repeat. Every punishment made me smarter, not better, more strategic about when and how to break rules. I learned the system's weak points the way a hacker learns code. It wasn't morality that guided me, it was efficiency. And yet, I still thought I was learning control. In reality, I was learning entropy. By fifteen, I'd already been caught again, this time not for a fight but for something calculated. Me and a few friends broke into classroom again, thinking we could outsmart the system by stealing computers and electronics. We were reckless, but we thought we were clever. We treated it like a heist movie. I hid the stolen gear in my closet, proud of the haul, like I'd actually accomplished something. But chaos doesn't reward pride. It exposes it. My mom found the school property tags on the equipment. She didn't yell. She didn't cry. She just picked up the phone and called my probation officer herself. That betrayal hit harder than any sentence. I understood it years later, but in that moment, it felt like my own blood had turned against me. The arrest that followed felt like deja vu, fingerprints, mugshots, handcuffs, the metallic echo of juvenile hall doors closing. The same loop playing out again. Each time I told myself this will be the last time, but the next variable always appeared, boredom, anger, desperation. It wasn't just rebellion anymore. It was addiction, not to a substance yet, but to stimulation. Chaos was my drug. The rush of defiance, the sense of movement, the illusion of control. I didn't need a bottle or a needle. I just needed to feel something. That's the thing no one tells you about the deadly sins. They don't start as corruption. They start as coping mechanisms. Greed starts as survival. Pride starts as self-respect. Lust starts as the need to be seen. They all come from hunger, until hunger turns to sickness. Every time I got locked up, the same thoughts played in my head. How did I get here again? Why do I keep doing this? But I never asked the real question. What am I running from? By sixteen, I was tired, not physically but spiritually. I'd been punished enough to know that punishment didn't heal anything. It only hardened the surface. The system never taught accountability, only compliance. There's a difference. Accountability comes from understanding. Compliance comes from fear. But even in the middle of that chaos, something in me was still observing. Every time I sat in a holding cell, staring at cracked paint and flickering lights, my mind would break down the system like a machine, intake, process, output. I'd trace where it failed, where it could be fixed. I didn't realize it then, but that was the same instinct that would later make me a technician, a systems thinker, a scientist. I didn't have faith yet, but I had analysis. And analysis, at least, kept me from going numb. That's the strange grace of suffering. When everything is stripped away, you start to see what's left, what's truly you. And what I saw back then wasn't pretty, but it was honest. A kid running on empty. A system overloaded. A human engine pushing past the redline, convinced it could handle the heat. But engines don't lie. And eventually, when they're pushed too far without calibration, they seize. I was seizing. I just didn't know it yet.

Run away

I was out of options, or at least that's what it felt like. Probation wasn't reforming me, school wasn't saving me, and home didn't feel like home. The system kept recycling me through the same loop, and every turn of the wheel stripped away a little more trust. So I did what every kid raised in chaos eventually tries. I ran. It wasn't random. It was a mission. I had recently tracked down my biological father online, a name and a profile buried in Myspace, the only platform where ghosts could still talk. He was real, alive, and living somewhere in Washington State. The man I'd built up in my head, the one who was supposed to explain everything, finally had a location. I thought if I could find him, maybe I'd find myself. Maybe I'd understand why I was wired this way, impulsive, restless, angry for no reason. Maybe I'd see what kind of man he really was and either learn from him or prove I was better. So, Stacie and I, who was now my girlfriend, decided to run away. We packed what little we had, scraped together money, and boarded a train heading north. I remember staring out the window as California blurred into Oregon, then Washington, the landscape shifting from desert to pine forest, the world outside looking cleaner, quieter, like maybe I could reboot everything if I just got far enough away. But the system doesn't let go that easily. We didn't even make it through the station before we were caught. As soon as we stepped off the train in Seattle, police were waiting. Someone had reported us. Her parents flew in the next day to take her home. I wasn't sent back right away. They brought me to the police station and sat me in a chair for hours, the fluorescent lights humming overhead, while I waited for a man I barely knew, my biological father, to pick me up. When he arrived, it wasn't the reunion I imagined. He didn't look like a savior. He looked like a man trying to survive his own collapse. Unshaven. Hollow-eyed. The smell of alcohol hit before his words did. He wasn't a father. He was a familiar pattern in a different body. Another system bleeding out under pressure. I wanted to believe it was still worth it. That maybe he'd tell me something I needed to hear, an explanation, a truth, a warning. But addicts don't offer guidance. They offer glimpses. And what I saw was enough, a mirror of everything I'd been running from. We stayed in touch for a short while, if you could call it that. His calls came at odd hours, slurred, fragmented. Sometimes he'd talk about regrets. Other times he'd talk in circles until passing out mid-sentence. I didn't know it yet, but I wasn't just looking at my father. I was looking at my own future if I didn't change something. It's strange how cycles hide inside families. They pass down like defective code, like generational entropy. You think you're different, but the same bugs show up under stress. That trip didn't heal anything. It just exposed the truth, the environment changes, but the core fracture stays unless you rebuild the structure itself. Free will versus determinism. I didn't have those words then, but I lived the paradox. Was I choosing chaos, or was I just replaying it? I was shipped back to California not long after, October 2007. Still on probation with thirty-eight years over my head, meaning I was put on probation instead of being sentenced to thirty-eight years in prison, as a plea deal. But I was back in the same loop. Different zip code. Same gravity. But that trip left something inside me, a splinter of clarity. I had gone over 1500 miles looking for a man who could explain my chaos, and all I found was proof that chaos doesn't explain itself. It just repeats until you decide to break the cycle. And at fifteen, I wasn't ready to break it yet. I still thought I could outrun it. What I didn't realize was that every time I ran, I was just tracing the same circle, one generation wide.

The Cycle Tightens

When I got back from Washington, I thought things might slow down. They didn't. I was fifteen, still on probation, still under constant watch, and still convinced I could bend the system if I just tried hard enough. But chaos doesn't bend, it coils. That's when Stacie came back into my life after I was released from juvenile hall again, but for the last time. Not as the girl who had run away with me, but as the girl who now lives around the corner because we moved again. It felt like something out of a movie, the kind of coincidence that made you think maybe the universe was giving you another shot. We started talking again. Slowly at first, then constantly. We weren't supposed to. Her parents had made that clear.

The restraining order had only made it clearer. But love, or what I thought was love back then, doesn't listen to legal boundaries. It doesn't see paperwork. It only sees what it wants to fix. And I thought if I could just hold onto her, if I could just keep that connection alive, everything else would make sense. That was the lie I told myself. Because underneath it, we were both broken kids looking for warmth in the same cold place. Her house was strict. Mine was fractured. We found balance in rebellion, sneaking out, hiding, meeting wherever we could. Every time someone tried to separate us, we pulled harder. The tension became the point. We mistook intensity for intimacy, conflict for proof that we cared. It's easy to romanticize dysfunction when it's the only kind you've ever known. When her parents finally got the restraining order, it felt like a betrayal written in legal ink. But really, it was just another line drawn between chaos and control, one I wasn't ready to respect. Every system has a feedback loop. Ours was powered by defiance. The more the world said no, the more I heard try harder. Looking back, that's when the cycle tightened. Attachment and neglect, push and pull, the same pattern I'd lived with my parents replaying itself in teenage form. She'd pull away, I'd chase. I'd mess up, she'd forgive. Then I'd mess up again, and she'd disappear. It wasn't love. It was survival with better lighting. At fifteen, I didn't know that yet. I thought passion meant pain. I thought intensity meant connection. I thought breaking rules meant loyalty. In truth, I was building another fracture, one I'd spend years trying to repair. We were two unstable systems colliding, generating more heat than light. The kind of bond that burns bright but doesn't last. Still, in that chaos, I felt alive. That's the paradox of duality. The same energy that destroys can also make you feel most real. And just like that, I was back where I'd always been, balancing on the fault line between freedom and consequence, between love and self-destruction, between who I was and who I was becoming. The cycle had tightened. And the next rupture was already forming.

Fault Line

I was sixteen when the ground shifted again. Cinco de Mayo, 2009. The day I found out I was going to be a father. The words hit like a fault line opening under my feet, silent at first, then seismic. For years I'd lived inside a loop of cause and effect I didn't fully understand. Courtrooms, probation officers, juvenile hall, each one another echo of the same mistake. But this was different. This wasn't a sentence from a judge. This was life itself handing me one. It terrified me more than any cell ever had. Thirty-eight years on paper didn't scare me like the idea of holding a newborn did. Jail was predictable. You knew the walls, the hours, the rules. But fatherhood, that was open sky and no map. Chaos had always been survivable when it was only me. But now survival wasn't enough. Now I had to become something more than reaction. I had to build. The truth was, I had nothing to build with. No license. No car. No job. No plan. All I had was curiosity, that same spark that had gotten me into trouble my entire life. The same thing that made me take apart radios, fix bikes, hack together ideas that half-worked. For the first time, it wasn't just a quirk. It was a tool. That instinct, to observe, to understand, to solve, became my survival code. If I didn't know how to do something, I could learn. If I didn't have a resource, I could create one. That's how the first emergent system in my life formed. Not from guidance or mentorship, but from necessity. From realizing that no one was coming to save me, and that I didn't need them to. Still, fear was constant. The future felt like standing on cracked glass, hearing it creak but not knowing where it would break. I remember lying awake some nights, staring at the ceiling, thinking, how am I supposed to raise a kid when I'm still trying to raise myself? But beneath the fear, something else flickered, a strange quiet resolve. The kind of hope that isn't loud or dramatic, but stubborn. The kind that says, if I can just hold this together one more day, maybe the pattern will break. That was the hope paradox in motion. I didn't suddenly become responsible or wise. I didn't even stop screwing up. But knowing someone else was tied to my choices changed the equation. For the first time, there was a variable in my system I couldn't ignore. It didn't fix me overnight. But it reprogrammed something deep inside. Survival started to mean more than just breathing. It meant building. Providing. Learning. The old system, chaos, rebellion, defiance, had reached its critical load. Fatherhood became the pressure test that forced a new system to form. And even though it would take years to understand, that moment was the pivot. The beginning of accountability. The first tremor of transformation. Because that's the truth about fault lines, they don't just destroy. They also reveal what's underneath.

Shockwave

When the news settled, you're going to be a father, the world didn't explode. It hummed. Quiet, steady, like an engine sitting idle before ignition. For months after, my life became a kind of slow-motion rebuild. Probation still hung over me. Money was thin. Every plan I made looked like scaffolding that could collapse at any moment. But under the noise, something subtle was shifting. The same chaos that used to burn through me now began to fuel me. I started seeing the chain reaction behind everything. Cause and effect. Load and response. Every decision pushed somewhere, on someone. If I skipped work, rent moved closer to overdue. If I blew a paycheck on liquor, groceries vanished. Every action had a reaction, and for the first time I cared about where the force landed. That was Newton's Third Law written into my own life, equal, opposite, unavoidable. There were still mistakes, plenty of them. Arguments. Missed calls. Nights I drank when I swore I wouldn't. But each failure left clearer data than the last. Every crack showed a stress point. Every consequence traced a line back to its source. That's when I began doing root cause analysis without knowing the term. If something broke, I wanted to know why. If I failed, I needed to map the chain that led there. It wasn't guilt, it was diagnostics. Pain became information. And information, if you study it long enough, becomes control. I started working harder. Fixing things instead of throwing them away. Small wins, tightening bolts, paying bills on time, keeping promises, stacked into quiet proof that order was possible. Every success felt like feedback from a system finally beginning to stabilize. Still, fear lingered. Not the fear of violence or arrest anymore, but of disappointing the small life that hadn't even arrived yet. It pressed on me like a constant vibration. But that vibration was energy too. It pushed me to act, to learn, to evolve. Looking back, that's what the shockwave really was, not an explosion outward, but an implosion inward, collapsing the old version of me to make room for something new. A recalibration. Entropy meeting design. I didn't know it then, but this was the moment when my survival instincts began transforming into engineering instincts. The first stirrings of the mind that would one day build rockets started here, in a cramped house living with my mom and stepdad, surrounded by bills and baby clothes, learning that chaos itself could be measured, mapped, and maybe even mastered. That realization was the first true pivot. The moment I stopped being a passenger inside my own disaster. From that point forward, I wasn't just reacting to life. I was beginning to build it.

Anchor Card

Paradox of Survival: *Endurance begins as adaptation, not wisdom.*

Principle: *Survival rewrites morality to preserve motion.*

Protocol: *Identify what you did to live, then ask what part of it still owns you.*

Proof: *Street instinct kept me alive but made peace impossible until truth rebuilt it.*

Observation logged

Chapter 2

Sparks and Systems

How ambition became combustion

Circuits of Control

Fatherhood hit like a fault line. The world did not explode, it split quietly underneath my feet. For years I had lived by reaction, a system without calibration. Anger, survival, instinct. The day I found out I was going to be a father, that wiring short circuited. I did not have money, a car, or even a license. What I had was fear and curiosity. The same instinct that once made me study chaos from the sidelines turned inward. If I could not escape my environment, maybe I could understand it. That is when I started building things. It began with computers, junk parts on a table, screws and boards that did not fit together yet. Most people saw scrap. I saw systems. Processors, motherboards, power supplies, circuits waiting for a pulse. Each part had a purpose even if it looked meaningless alone. When I powered up that first build, it was more than a machine booting up. It was proof. Cause and effect were finally obeying me. For the first time, the world responded exactly as I designed it to. I learned fast. Voltage, airflow, heat, it all followed rules. You did not need luck or mercy. You needed math, patience, and flow. When something failed, there was always a reason. The system was not broken, I was missing something. That realization rewired my brain. I stopped seeing life as random. Every failure had a pattern. Every outcome had a traceable cause. That was root cause analysis again before I ever knew the term. At first I built out of need. Then I built out of pride. The first time a circuit actually worked, I felt it in my chest before I saw it. The bulb flickered, then glowed steady, a soft pulse of light that seemed alive. The smell of warm metal filled the room. For a moment I just watched the wire hum with current, the same way I used to watch gears move on my bike as a kid. The joy wasn't just in the light itself. It was in the logic behind it, the precision that made it possible. That feeling, the perfect alignment between cause and effect, became my first high. When it burned out a second later, I laughed. Not out of frustration, but out of awe. Creation and collapse always came as a pair. Word spread fast, friends and gamers started coming to me for rigs. They wanted systems that ran smoother and faster than store bought ones. I optimized voltage, overclocked processors, rerouted airflow, small changes that made massive differences. It felt like alchemy. Take raw materials, silicon, copper, code, and breathe order into them. Creation out of chaos. Deep down, that touched something ancient in me, the same drive that makes an engineer stare at broken things until they work. Looking back, I first brushed against Newton's third law. For every action, an equal and opposite reaction. In life I had spent years absorbing other people's actions, violence, judgment, chaos. Now I was finally pushing back. Every build was a counterforce to the disorder I came from. But control can be intoxicating. Every time I fixed something I felt a spark, not just pride but power. For the first time nothing else mattered, not probation, not fear, not the weight of who I used to be. I was in control. Money started to flow. Not a lot, but enough to feel like freedom, and that was new and dangerous in its own way. When you grow up counting coins for food, cash feels like oxygen. In the wrong environment oxygen does not heal, it fuels fire. I started spending fast. New clothes, gadgets, amusement parks, trips, things I had never had. It was not luxury. It was compensation. I was feeding the part of me that had gone hungry too long. In psychology they call it overcorrection. In physics it is still energy transfer, moving power from one broken circuit to another. The energy that once drove survival had become consumption, and like every overloaded system I did not see the imbalance until something started to smoke. Still, underneath the mistakes, a pattern was forming. Each computer I built was a small act of creation. Every success was data. The more I observed, the more I realized that complexity was not chaos, it was order waiting to be decoded. That was my first glimpse of emergent properties, how simple actions repeated with precision create intelligence. Every screw I tightened, every wire I routed, every voltage I tuned combined into something greater than its parts. It was not just a machine anymore. It was a mirror, showing me that life could work the same way. Small consistent actions.

Proper inputs. Energy balanced through discipline. The laws did not change between physics and faith, only the language did. Back then I did not have the vocabulary. I just knew nothing breaks for no reason, and nothing works without order. That is what I was chasing, not money or status, but order. For a while it looked like I had found it. The thing about systems is this, once you control one you start believing you can control them all. That illusion followed me for years, from engines to rockets to relationships, the idea that understanding something means mastering it. It always ends the same way. Eventually the current finds resistance. When it does, something burns.

Fuel and Fire

When the current moved from wires to engines, everything changed. Computers were quiet and obeyed logic. Engines talked back. They shook the ground. They breathed. They felt alive in a way circuitry never could. My first car was not a project, it was a rescue. A trade gone sideways. I traded a home theater system of all things, for a 97 Grand Cherokee which basically left me with a wreck that barely idled, coughing oil and smoke like it wanted to die. I had no money to fix it, no tools worth owning, and no training. I had the same equation in my head. If it is broken there is a reason. Find it. Fix it. I started small, a spark plug swap, a belt replacement, oil black as tar. Every bolt I broke loose was a variable solved. Every successful start was proof that chaos could be forced into rhythm. I spent days in parking lots and auto parts aisles, reading manuals like scripture. The employees at Pep Boys learned my face before they learned my name. At first they humored me, another broke kid asking questions. Then they noticed I kept coming back with answers. One of them offered me a job. It felt like my first real promotion, not a court ordered role or a scam for cash, but earned ground. On that concrete floor, with grease under my nails and heat bleeding through my clothes, I found my new classroom. The logic of mechanics was elemental. Air, fuel, spark. Compression, ignition, exhaust. Balance or failure. Every misfire had a reason. Every success a sequence. If computers taught me precision, engines taught me humility. You can do everything right, torque every bolt to spec, and still have something seize. Physics does not care about pride. Neither does combustion. I loved it. The smell of gasoline, the hum of a tuned motor, the feedback of torque through a wrench, it was meditation through motion. At Pep Boys I learned speed. At Firestone I learned command. I was not just fixing cars anymore. I was leading people. Scheduling, diagnosing, selling, calming angry customers while holding the line with my crew. Leadership came the same way engineering had, by observation. I watched how energy flowed through a team. If the manager panicked, everyone followed. If I stayed calm, the shop stayed stable. That was my first taste of group dynamics and leadership energy, how one person's tone can set the vibration for ten others. It was resonance in human form. Duality lived in the background. The harder I worked, the harder I played. When the shop closed, I poured whiskey. The same hands that aligned suspension and balanced tires were pouring until dawn. Each drink felt earned, fuel for the engine that never stopped running. It was not fuel. It was corrosion. Work was order. Drinking was entropy. Day built what night dismantled. I told myself it balanced out, creation and destruction. It was a lie, but a convincing one. Every morning I still showed up, hit the quotas, and outperformed everyone around me. That illusion of control was intoxicating. By the time I moved to Firestone full time I was running the place. Tire bays, diagnostics, sales, operations, all of it. Customers trusted me because I spoke truth instead of script. If something was not worth fixing, I said so. If it was, I explained why. The business thrived. While the shop hummed, I was burning out. Late nights turned into blackouts. Arguments turned into slammed doors. The stronger my outer system became, the weaker the inner one grew. Looking back, that period was an equation written in fire. Energy transfer plus duality equals combustion. Every ounce of drive that built my career came from the same reservoir that fueled my addiction. The two were never separate systems. They shared a tank, and every success I poured in increased the pressure. I did not know it then, but this was my first real load test, the point where the structure starts to hum under stress. Every hum is a warning.

Telemetry Insert

Thermal Signal Spike

Input: *Continuous motion without rest. The rhythm of ambition exceeded safe operating range.*

State: *Rising temperature, ego masking exhaustion.*

Output: *Burnout threshold approaching, system integrity compromised.*

Observation logged

Load Bearing

Success does not always announce itself with applause. Sometimes it creeps in quietly, disguised as workload. Firestone was that kind of success. What began as a mechanic's job turned into management, then into responsibility that bled into every waking hour. I ran the shop like a control room. Every bay, every tech, every customer ticket ran through me. If one sensor was off, one miscommunication, one bad torque reading, one unhappy customer, the whole system trembled. I learned to feel pressure the way a machine feels load, not as panic but as vibration. If you listen closely enough, every system hums before it breaks. On the surface I was thriving. The numbers were good. The team respected me. Corporate noticed. What no one saw was that I was not sleeping. I was drinking at night, running diagnostics by day, and patching holes faster than I could count them. That was the beginning of the expectation paradox. The more capable I became, the more was demanded of me. Every solved problem became proof I could handle more. Every success raised the floor of what normal looked like. Every ounce of approval became fuel for another overextension. Customers came in angry and left calm. My crew burned out and I took their shifts. Someone quit and I absorbed their workload. The load kept growing and I mistook endurance for strength. Load bearing structures do not fail when you add weight once. They fail under repetition. It is not the heaviest moment that cracks you. It is the constant vibration over time. At work I had structure. At home it was entropy. My relationship was slipping into resentment. I was too tired to engage and too prideful to admit it. The more I succeeded outside, the more I failed inside. That is when the great filter began, not cosmic but personal. The universe has a way of separating what can evolve from what cannot. For civilizations it is technology outpacing morality. For me it was ambition outpacing wisdom. The stronger I became professionally, the more spiritually hollow I felt. Everyone faces a narrowing gate where ego, addiction, and denial either burn away or harden into a ceiling. I kept doubling down. When corporate rolled out new targets, I crushed them. When other managers burned out, I covered. I started believing I could outwork entropy itself. It was resilience, but the wrong kind. Resilience through suffering without reflection is slow collapse. It is the illusion of progress while the system corrodes inside. The illusion had rewards. Paychecks grew. My name circulated. Recruiters called. One opportunity led to another, until I stepped into a different hangar, Parker Aerospace. The transition felt almost spiritual. Firestone was noise. Parker was precision. Clean floors, quiet rooms, tight tolerances. Here a tenth of a millimeter meant failure. The tools were sharper, the margins thinner, the consequences greater. For a while I felt reborn. I traded rubber and oil for pumps and actuators. I started thinking in terms of force distribution, yield stress, and fatigue cycles, principles that mirrored my life more than I realized. I was still in load testing. Every test stand and every actuator under pressure was a sermon. Apply stress, record deflection, watch for cracks. It was what I had been doing my whole life, just in a refined environment. At Parker I learned that resilience is not only withstanding stress, it is knowing the threshold where adaptation begins. Push too little, you never evolve. Push too much, you break. The sweet spot between chaos and control is where mastery lives. I had not mastered myself. I still thought resilience meant carrying everything, never letting go, never showing weakness. The system of me was all tensile strength and no flexibility. Metal that does not flex does not survive the quake. That belief followed me into my next chapter. At SpaceX it would be tested beyond anything I knew. Every system has a breaking point. I was about to find mine.

The Catalyst

Every system has a moment where pressure stops destroying and starts transforming. At Parker Aerospace that moment began quietly, not with applause or promotion, but with a question that would not leave my mind. Why does this work? Most people were content to follow procedures, torque this to spec, check that value, move on. I wanted to know why the spec existed, why a tolerance mattered, why the system behaved the way it did under load. Every test, every actuator, every data line became an equation begging for interpretation. That question was the ignition spark. It was the same curiosity that got me in trouble as a kid, now redirected into structure. Instead of chaos, I was decoding systems. Instead of breaking rules to feel control, I learned the rules so deeply I could bend them toward improvement. Out of thousands of small, repetitive actions, calibration, analysis, adjustment, a larger intelligence formed. My mind became a feedback loop of cause and effect, pattern and consequence. Without realizing it, I was engineering myself. People talk about manifestation as thoughts creating outcomes. Physics says it simply. For every action there is an equal and opposite reaction. You do not manifest through wishful thinking. You manifest through alignment. When thoughts, actions, and intent resonate at the same frequency, reality responds with precision. That is Newton's law in the language of faith. The motion you set in one realm ripples through the others. My curiosity turned into competence. Competence into confidence. Confidence into opportunity. What once felt accidental became mechanical. I was not surviving entropy anymore. I was using it. I became known for solving problems faster than expected. If a test sequence failed, I did not just reset it. I mapped it. If a hydraulic line leaked, I did not just patch it. I traced the stress concentration that caused it. Going beyond the obvious started drawing attention. It was not luck. It was resonance. The system was responding to the energy I fed it. Every force creates its counterforce. The more control I gained professionally, the less I had emotionally. At home, friction built. My marriage was a pressure vessel with no release valve. I was still drinking, still numbing, still thinking I could manage entropy in one domain while ignoring it in another. Free will and determinism coexist like thrust and drag. You have freedom to move, but you move within the medium you have already built. Every choice carries the momentum of the ones before it. Every trajectory is shaped by prior vectors. I was operating under forces I had not fully understood yet, generational, emotional, spiritual. I kept pushing forward. One night scrolling through aerospace forums and job boards I saw it. SpaceX is hiring. The words hit differently. Not because I thought I was qualified, but because it felt like gravity. Everything I had done, curiosity, pattern recognition, load bearing, obsession, had trained me for something I did not know existed. I did not apply out of ambition. I applied out of inevitability. When the interview came, the air felt charged, like the system had aligned. Every failure and fracture had been building toward that ignition. Parker had been the fuel. SpaceX would be the flame. When the offer came, I did not hesitate. I left stability for chaos, and this time it was deliberate. I wanted to test the limits of everything I had learned about pressure, precision, and perseverance. That leap was my catalyst event. The moment my life stopped being about surviving entropy and started being about mastering it. I did not know it yet, but that transition would become the crucible for every paradox I had studied, faith and physics, sin and symmetry, chaos and control. SpaceX was not just a company. It was a mirror, and everything I had been running from was waiting for me inside it.

Engines of Fire

When I first walked into SpaceX it did not feel like a company. It felt like a living organism. The air vibrated with motion. Machines hummed, forklifts weaved, tools clattered in organized chaos. You could feel the frequency, not noise but resonance. Everyone was tuned to the same wavelength, precision under pressure. I did not just want to be part of it. I wanted to understand its rhythm. I already knew systems, but here I learned combustion. Every piece, metal, software, human, carried a vibration that either harmonized with the mission or disrupted it. You could see it in posture, pace, and breath. There was no room for hesitation. Hesitation was entropy. I started in composites test, setting up and running structural qualification tests for carbon fiber components like fairings, landing legs, interstages, raceway covers, and heat shields. My job was to simulate what rockets endure through launch, ascent, descent, and landing, thousands of pounds of pressure, vibration, and heat. Each test was a small version of the universe, order under load with chaos waiting to break through. I was living the metaphor. Each test was me, pushed to failure, rebuilt, and pushed again. Each fracture was a reflection. We simulated flight conditions, ascent torque, landing impact, and thermal expansion, and I saw how everything left a signature. When a structure failed, it was not random. There were patterns, strain drops, fiber splits, and microfractures forming before the audible crack. You can see collapse coming if you are sensitive to the frequency. That is resonant frequency. Every structure, physical or spiritual, has a point where the load aligns with its natural vibration. If the frequency matches, it amplifies until it breaks. In rockets that is destructive resonance. In humans it is burnout. At work I was addicted to that edge. The hum of hydraulics, the smell of carbon fiber under tension, the feeling of data coming alive, it was pure flow. For those long nights I was tuned perfectly. Focused, aligned, alive. The resonance followed me home. My body stayed wired. My mind raced while the world slept. I poured a drink to dampen the frequency, to lower the amplitude, not realizing I was teaching my system to burn cleaner in chaos than in calm. That is energy transfer. Nothing disappears. It shifts form. The energy I could not resolve at work had to go somewhere, and home became the outlet. Precision on the clock. Destruction off it. I thrived in the mission. SpaceX did not care where you came from. It cared what you could do under load. My past did not matter. My lack of a degree did not matter. The test in front of me mattered. If I could build it, test it, or fix it faster and better than the next person, I was trusted. That meritocracy was oxygen. I learned to collapse time. Where others needed weeks, I found ways to compress to days and sometimes hours. I became the only person to test a full flight set of landing legs by myself in one shift. What should have taken a team weeks, I finished before dawn. It was not just obsession. It was orchestration. Every tool, process, and calculation synced like a metronome in my head. I did not feel human. I felt mechanical, perfectly calibrated. Perfection is expensive. The better I performed, the more the system demanded. If there was a gap, I filled it. If a test stalled, I stayed. Night shift became my shift. I became the anchor, the constant when everything else rotated. People said,

Giavelli will handle it. That is group dynamics. Leadership not by title but by energy. On nights the crew mirrored whoever set the pace. If I came in focused, they locked in. If I was off, the floor felt it. Energy is contagious. A leader's emotional resonance spreads through the system faster than vibration through metal. That responsibility carried weight. As I rose, my home life fell. The energy I gave the mission drained what little was left of me. I told myself I was doing it for family, security, pride, legacy. The truth was simpler. I was feeding one fire to starve another. The paradox of engines of fire is creation and destruction powered by the same fuel. The drive that launched rockets was destroying me. The focus that made me indispensable was making me absent. The precision that built aerospace perfection was dismantling human connection. I could not stop. When you find a place that mirrors your chaos and turns your madness into purpose, it is almost impossible to walk away. SpaceX was more than work. It was worship. Not of rockets, but of order. A cathedral of fire where I could atone for mistakes through output. If I could work hard enough and fast enough and perfectly enough, maybe I could burn away everything I hated about myself. Entropy always collects its debt. No system runs forever without calibration. My calibration point was coming, and when it did it would not just shake the walls of the test stand. It would shake everything I had built.

Anchor Card

Law of Combustion: *Heat is information, pain is pressure announcing imbalance.*

Principle: *Excess energy without purpose becomes destruction.*

Protocol: *Reduce load, recalibrate intent, reroute pressure into creation.*

Proof: *The engine that nearly failed became the teacher that defined endurance.*

Observation logged

Chapter 3

Engines of Fire

Pressure becomes instruction

Resonant Flow

SpaceX did not just change the way I worked, it changed the way I moved. Every night when I walked into the test lab I could feel the pulse in the walls. The air was charged with static and adrenaline. Machines whined, compressors hissed, data streamed across monitors like living veins. The building felt alive, breathing in effort and exhaling heat, and it did not take long before I matched its rhythm. My hands, my thoughts, my movements, everything fell into sync. I was not working anymore, I was flowing. People talk about purpose like it is something you think about, but here purpose was something you felt in your bones. Every wrench turn, every torque click, every vibration that ran through the concrete meant something. The resonance was not just mechanical, it was spiritual. The closer a test came to the edge of failure, the closer I felt to the truth. That is resonance in its purest form. When two frequencies align, their energy amplifies. The test stand had its vibration and I had mine, and together we hummed. Some people chase that feeling in religion, others in addiction, I found it in work. Flow is seductive. It feels holy, like you are touching something larger than yourself. You stop feeling pain, you stop feeling hunger, hours pass without a thought, and you do not just perform, you become the performance. The machine and the man blur into one system. That is when I realized work could be worship, and in a way it was. In the middle of all that noise and speed, there were moments of unspoken understanding. A glance across the test bay. A nod before a lift. A hand signal that meant trust without a single word. Those seconds of human synchronization were the purest form of resonance I had ever felt. The machinery ran on data, but the team ran on something harder to define. Every torque, every calibration, every clean run carried an invisible pulse of belonging. It wasn't friendship. It was flow. Every act of precision and every clean test felt like redemption. The more flawless the data, the quieter my mind became, as if I could erase the chaos of my past one calibration at a time. But worship without wisdom burns too hot. The flow state is fragile. You cannot live inside it forever. It is like flight, sustained only by thrust, and when the thrust fades you fall. I did not notice it at first. The fatigue, the irritability, the headaches were easy to ignore when your entire identity is tied to performance. Underneath the flow something else was building. Stress is not just mental. It is vibrational. It accumulates in muscles, nerves, and thoughts. Every system has a natural frequency, and when pushed too long that frequency turns destructive. I had tuned myself so perfectly to chaos that I did not know how to live without it. If the floor was quiet I got restless. If systems ran too smoothly I started looking for what could go wrong. I thrived on pressure spikes, anomalies, and alarms. They made me feel alive. It was not adrenaline, it was identity. My life became a waveform, high amplitude at work and low flat silence at home, a constant oscillation between meaning and nothing. That is what burnout really is, not exhaustion but imbalance, pushing so hard in one direction that your system cannot recover between cycles. I kept going because that resonance gave me something nothing else had, belonging. In a world that always felt chaotic this was the first place where chaos had rules and I could master them. I began to equate divine order with performance, thinking God could be reached through mastery, control, and flawless execution. Perfection is not divinity, it is imitation, and imitation always cracks. My crack had not surfaced yet. I was still humming, sharp, precise, and relentless, but every resonance has a limit, and mine was approaching fast.

The Few Who Stayed

There is a moment in every mission when theory gives way to urgency, when the data stops being numbers and starts being consequence. For me that moment came on a night when reviewing strain gauge data, there was a story no one wanted to hear. We were deep into testing a completely different fairing when something was noticed. A pattern, small strain drops that should not have existed. Carbon fiber does not behave that way unless something inside is starting to separate. Debonding. Hidden damage. No one wanted to believe it. The fairings were supposed to be perfect, problem was, it matched data for flight hardware already bound for the Cape, but numbers do not lie and carbon does not forgive wishful thinking. If there was even a chance the readings were real we had to know. The decision came fast. Retest everything. Bring the fairings back. Both halves. Rush order. I waited as the fairings got flown in by the Antonov, that massive cargo plane dwarfing everything around it, hangar doors opening as the fairings rolled out like sleeping giants. Most people had gone home for the holiday. Thanksgiving week. A few of us stayed. The ones who lived in the rhythm of pressure and deadlines. We did not talk much. Just nods and unspoken trust. We set up the stands, connected actuators, wired sensors, calibrated every channel, then drove full structural loads, launch, ascent, and atmospheric stress. Hours of cycling, data streaming, pumps whining like an unbroken heartbeat. The clock stopped meaning anything. Wednesday bled into Thursday. Night into morning. Sweat, heat, caffeine, and silence. When it was done the data was clean. No strain drops. No hidden damage. The mission could fly. I stepped outside into sunrise, body aching like metal under stress, hands raw, eyes burning. Thanksgiving had come and gone. I stood in the lot looking up, thinking about the arc those fairings would follow, the same arc I had simulated for hours. Missing the holiday did not feel like loss. It felt like purpose.

Obsession does not feel like sacrifice when you believe the work matters more than you do. That night was not just about the test. It was about the people who stayed, the few who carry the load when everyone else goes home. The same drive that nearly ended me in South Texas had a home here. The stubbornness that wrecked relationships also built rockets. The energy was the same, only the aim changed. Energy is never evil by itself. What you aim it toward defines it. That night I aimed higher than myself and it held. Purpose without rest is still imbalance, and balance, like structure, only bends so far before it breaks.

Condensed Time

At SpaceX time did not move in days. It moved in deliverables. Weeks blurred into cycles of tests, rebuilds, and launches. There were no weekends, only countdowns. The system did not reward endurance, it required it. If you could not outlast the load, someone else would. I adapted. I learned to live without rest and then I learned to condense everything. What took a team weeks I finished in days. What took days I finished in hours. I was not cutting corners. I was cutting waste. Every repetition and process I mapped and stripped to essentials. Once I saw the pattern I could not unsee it. Efficiency became instinct. I woke up with setups already assembled in my head, parameters, load cycles, fixture layouts, all lining up like code compiling itself. I tested a full flight set of Falcon 9 landing leg actuators and A arms by myself, work that normally took a crew weeks, done in a day. Alone. No shortcuts. Just pace, precision, and focus. That was my high, not the alcohol, not the praise, but the moment when physics, time, and endurance bent to will. People noticed the output but not the cost. When I condensed time, I mortgaged the future for the present. Every win charged interest. Hours stolen from sleep, meals skipped, aches ignored, all built up like unseen stress in a composite panel. Composites hide damage until it is too late. Night shift magnified everything. The world slept while I worked in a twilight between exhaustion and clarity. Pumps whined, hydraulics groaned, data hummed. The controlled chaos and the hum of readiness mirrored something inside me. If the world outside was disorder, this was order I could command. Obsession does not feel like madness from the inside. It feels like clarity. Locked in that deep, every variable matters and every motion has purpose. It feels holy. Holiness without humility becomes its own kind of sin. The higher I climbed the more invisible the cost became. The late arrivals stopped. The write ups were gone. I was a machine again, tuned and productive. When you bend time, you bend yourself. Something eventually gives. I did not see it. I felt only the output and the hum, the peace that lives right before something breaks.

Cracks in the Armor

Cracks do not arrive all at once. They start as whispers, a small delay, a foggy thought, a half step slower than yesterday. I told myself I was fine, that exhaustion was part of the grind and I could push through like always. Then the edges frayed. I would tighten a fitting or read data and realize I could not remember if I had logged a step. My hands moved while my mind lagged. I caught small mistakes and corrected them before anyone noticed, and their existence gnawed at me. My body started throwing alarms. Muscles twitched, eyes burned, hands cramped, and I kept moving because the schedule does not stop for pain. High performance systems hide degradation behind output. As long as the numbers look good, no one checks the bearings. Someone finally did. A supervisor pulled me aside, calm and direct. You have been late, not often, but enough that people notice. It was not the lateness that hit me, it was the word people. For years I had been the constant, the closer, the person who carried load no one else would touch. Now I was a risk factor. He was right. I had started slipping. Nights at home were blurring. Bottles had reentered the rotation, one to unwind, then two, then more. I tightened up the optics, stopped being late, and fixed the surface. No more write ups. On paper I was solid. Reliability on paper is not stability in reality. The drinking did not stop. It moved. Where I once showed cracks at work, I learned to contain them at home. Damage hid behind closed doors. That is the illusion of control. You think if you isolate a failure to one subsystem the machine can still function. Isolation is a myth. Pressure equalizes. I would drive home watching the sunrise and feel proof of imbalance, everyone waking up while I shut down. The silence inside my front door was heavy. Some mornings I'd find Kage half asleep in his room waiting for me, blanket half pulled over his shoulders, playstation still playing. He'd wake up, grin, and say, "Your home! Good morning!" Just those words cut through everything the noise at work couldn't. I'd nod, too tired to speak, and he'd go back to playing. That was the only part of the day that felt right. The few quiet minutes before sleep and guilt set in. It was the last working circuit in a house I was slowly shorting out. My wife and my son were sleeping when I got home most of the time, our lives moved in opposite directions, barely intersecting. The distance was not just emotional. It was orbital. What I had built was not balance. It was duality. One world that thrived on precision and one that rotted in silence. Both were me. Both were true. I was running out of room between them. Performance covered the noise but never changed the signal. At work I was a closed loop, measure, correct, repeat. At home I was an open loop, react, regret, repeat. That gap did not scare me yet. It should have.

The Illusion of Control

For years I believed control was strength. If I could outwork the problem, outthink the system, and outlast the failure, I was winning. In the hangar that was true. You can take a failing actuator, rebuild it, tune the parameters, and make it work. Cause and effect. Logic and output. Outside the hangar life does not obey those rules. You cannot torque a relationship to spec. You cannot bleed a soul for trapped air. You cannot replace faith like a faulty valve. I still tried. Every drink was calibration. Every argument was data I thought I could model. Every silence between me and Stacie became a simulation I believed I could fix later, when I had time. Time is a system with limits. You cannot stretch it without paying. Control is not strength. Control is fear dressed well. It is the refusal to trust anything outside your own hands. I was not only addicted to alcohol. I was addicted to control. The bottle was the lever I used to make reality feel manageable. One sip and the noise dimmed. One more and the world felt predictable again. It worked until it did not. At work I could still deliver. At home my systems failed without warning. No alarms. No diagnostics. Just fallout. Conversations turned to static. Meals turned to silence. Nights turned to escape routes, not away from her but away from myself. It was entropy disguised as order, slow decay hidden behind clean metrics. If you ignore pressure it does not vanish. It relocates. At SpaceX pressure meant performance. At home it was poison. You cannot vent it or ground it or analyze it away. You face it or it ruptures everything you love. I was not ready to face it. I told myself a story that made sense to the systems thinker in me, that as long as the system kept producing output it was not failing. The logic I used to save hardware was killing my humanity. Delusion hides inside a truth. I thought I was holding everything together. I was managing decay. Like any overloaded system I was heading toward critical failure. I could feel the hum of instability, the faint vibration before resonance turns destructive. Illusion does not shatter in one moment. It fades piece by piece until one day you realize it is gone. When mine broke it did not break at work. It broke at home, far from Hawthorne, in South Texas, where every crack I had ignored finally connected and the system I built collapsed under its own weight.

Anchor Card

Resonant Failure: *The hum before collapse is warning disguised as rhythm.*

Principle: *Systems announce decay before breaking.*

Protocol: *Listen for repetition, silence proves disconnection.*

Proof: *The test stand's vibration mirrored my own overdrive. Both signaled fracture.*

Observation logged

Pattern detected

Chapter 4

The Break Point

When structure yields to mercy

Pressure Test

Texas was supposed to be a reset, a clean start, a quieter world where I could work, breathe, and rebuild the pieces that SpaceX had sharpened and alcohol had dulled. I accepted a new position at SpaceX in Starship Flight Operations that moved me to South Texas in September of 2020 after visiting several times. It felt like a new beginning, where I once felt like exile. I traded smaller test stands for silence, hangars for fields, and purpose for space. At first the silence felt pure, even therapeutic. I told myself it was peace, but it was only the absence of noise, and absence is not the same as healing. The land stretched flat and still. Canals did not move. Heat and diesel hung in the air. Everything looked alive but paused, like God had stopped the frame mid scene. I worked nonstop. Fixed fences, hauled debris, dug trenches. It was mechanical, not mindful, busy hands to keep thoughts from catching up. That is what addicts do when they stop feeding the addiction. If you cannot drink the chaos, you build it. For a few weeks I convinced myself it was working. The hangover fog lifted. My body steadied. My hands stopped shaking in the morning. Without noise there was only data. Every memory, every mistake, every avoided conversation replayed like telemetry from a failed launch. It became a pressure test. You think you are fine until the structure groans. There is a moment right before a failure when a frame holds more load than it should. Bolts stretch, welds flex, the system has not broken yet but you can hear it deciding whether to. That was me. I prayed in the morning, worked through the day, collapsed at night. It looked like discipline. It was avoidance dressed as structure. The evening before it all gave way was strangely calm. South Texas light spread gold across the yard, long shadows stretching over the gravel like cables before tension. The wind had slowed, the humidity finally dropping after weeks of heat. I remember the sound of the distant highway, the muffled rhythm of engines coming and going. For once, the world wasn't asking anything of me. I sat on the back steps with a fruit smoothie and just watched the sky fade from orange to gray. The cicadas started their chorus and the air felt still enough to measure. For a few minutes there was no pressure, no noise, no deadlines. Just a still system holding perfect equilibrium before the next vibration. Looking back, I think God gives us those moments right before collapse, not as warnings, but as grace. A breath before the break. A reminder that peace existed, even if only to show us what we were about to lose. The pressure kept rising. Isolation changes time. Days blend. Nights echo. Reference points disappear. One evening I heard myself answering questions out loud to no one and realized I had not spoken to another person in days. In that quiet something darker started whispering again. It was not only temptation. It was invitation. You have earned it. One drink will not matter. You work harder than anyone. You deserve a break. The same voice that once promised control now promised comfort. I tried to drown it with work, with logic, with prayer. Willpower does not silence a demon. It delays him. When the first bottle came back into the house it felt like relief, not relapse. That is how addiction hides. Not as rebellion, but as mercy. The system had not failed yet, but the pressure was climbing and I could hear the structure creaking. The silence that followed felt heavier than the noise ever did. No shouting. No motion. Just air thick with the smell of alcohol and regret. I sat there watching what was left, trying to piece together the seconds that had vanished. Nothing rewound. Nothing apologized. The scene was still. For the first time in a long time, I saw everything exactly as it was. It was ugly, but the system told the truth. Every broken thing in that room was data. Every bruise, every silence, every shattered object had meaning. I could finally read it. God had stripped away every excuse until all that was left was cause and effect. I was not cursed. I was accountable.

System Degradation

The drinking returned slowly. A sip at night to quiet static, then two, then a bottle open on the counter before noon. I called it balance. I was not drunk at work, I was not missing deadlines. I was fixing things, maintaining the property, doing something. Function is not health. A machine can run long after it starts breaking down. The land became an echo chamber. Every creak in the wall and groan in the wind sounded like voices, not loud enough to understand, just enough to remind me I was not alone even when I wanted to be. Alcohol stopped being a habit. It became a habitat. Morning recovery, afternoon maintenance, evening relapse, a loop like a feedback circuit without a resistor. The longer I lived in it the more my body mirrored the systems I had tested all my life, stressed, fatigued, leaking pressure. My skin went gray. My eyes burned. My heart skipped. Hangovers settled into bone. Addiction does not scream. It whispers the same line, you can fix this tomorrow. Tomorrow never comes. It resets slightly worse than the day before. My wife stopped trying to talk through it. Conversations became deflection or blame. Silences became resentment. We lived like cohabitants, not partners. I knew the equations, cause, effect, consequence, but logic does not save you from decay. It lets you diagnose it while you rot. I felt the corruption move through me like rust through metal. Chest tight on the inhale. Stomach burned after every pour. Thoughts fragmented, looping like corrupted files. I started thinking in data again. Each symptom a readout. Each failure telemetry. The system was degrading in real time and I could not stop watching. That is the trap. Observation is not repentance. You

cannot analyze your way out of sin. You surrender it or
you serve it. I was not ready to surrender. I compensated.
More caffeine, less food, more alcohol, less sleep. The
load stayed the same and tolerance dropped. Entropy
does not care how smart you are. It only cares how long
you resist the inevitable. By then I had crossed the line
between using and being used. The alcohol was no longer
an escape from a demon. It was the demon. I felt it every
time I poured, that faint electric pulse in my gut that said
this is not you. The corrosion spread. Faith became
theory. Hope turned into background noise. The man
who analyzed rocket microfractures could not see the
cracks forming inside his own soul.

Critical Load

There is a point where pressure stops being data and
becomes prophecy. You feel it in the air, silence heavier
than sound, even your thoughts echo too loud. Life in
Texas became one long stress test. Work did not end and
did not fix anything. At home, mowing, repairing, digging
kept my hands busy and my head quiet, and the quiet
turned dangerous. It was not silence. It was listening. The
land felt like it was waiting to see which part of me would
fail first. Load built from small things that compounded
into something structural. Arguments that started
nowhere and went nowhere. Half sleep at night.
Mornings staring in the mirror to see if anything inside
was still alive. My wife spoke in measured words, like she

was handling something volatile. I did not blame her. I was volatile, pressurized, unpredictable, ready to detonate over nothing. The alcohol no longer calmed me. It turned me into static. I could feel it rewiring my brain, dulling conscience and feeding impulse. One moment I was fine, the next I was pacing the house and inventing reasons to be angry. Addiction does not only rot the soul. It rewrites the code. Empathy runs backward. Love reads as threat. Truth becomes noise. God feels like He is on the other side of a sealed bulkhead, present but not intervening. I still prayed sometimes, half drunk and half broken, pacing in the dark. The words were fractured, part plea, part curse, part noise. God does not always answer panic. Sometimes He waits for surrender. I was not there. I still thought I could outwork the collapse. Things would get better once I slept more, once we talked more, once I slowed down. Every variable depended on me, and I was the failure mode. The air felt charged, like the seconds before lightning. Walking past my wife felt like wading through static. Looking at my son hurt in a way I did not have vocabulary for. A dark thought began to whisper, the same one from Moreno Valley, you are not worth saving. At first I argued. Then I agreed. Despair does not need to convince you. It only needs to exhaust you. The night it broke there was no big trigger. No explosion. Just the slow snap of a man who ran out of corrections to apply. You do not notice the exact moment a system crosses the failure line. It feels like every other moment until it does not, and once it happens there is no rewind. Only aftermath. That is when the sheriff came, and mercy arrived wearing a badge.

Failure Event

Blackouts do not feel like sleep. They feel like someone editing your memory in real time, cutting frames and leaving static. That night exists in flashes, not a story. I remember the house humming with tension, my voice raised without knowing the words. I remember movement, my wife, my son, shadows at the edge of vision. I remember the sound of my heartbeat, loud and hollow. Then blank. The next frame is blue and red light washing the walls. Officers in the yard. Voices sharp and clipped. My body moving while I watched from somewhere behind my own eyes. I heard myself arguing, words slurred, anger automatic. I had always distrusted police. Authority, uniforms, lectures. In my head they blurred together. Even through the blur I knew this was bad. They were not here to check in. They were ready to take me. Then a familiar voice cut in. The sheriff. He had been to the house before. He heard the call and came himself. Not because he had to, because he remembered me. He stepped between me and the officers. Calm. Direct. I will take over from here. The others did not like it. They wanted to haul me in. He held the line. I can still see Stacie behind them. Silent. Exhausted. She could have asked them to take me. She did not. Her face said it clearly. This is not forgiveness. This is mercy. The sheriff matched it. No sugarcoating. He told me the truth. I was at the edge. This was a last chance. I do not remember what I said. I remember my hands shaking and a weight in my gut, shame mixed with relief. The lights faded. The cruisers left. The sheriff left. The house went quiet. That night did not save me or make me sober or erase damage. It exposed me. It showed me a version of myself I could not rationalize away, violent, drunk, and somehow spared. Grace came from two directions, my wife and the sheriff, and I did not deserve either. It is one thing to survive your own chaos. It is another to see people stand between you and consequences you earned. I am thankful the sheriff was there. He was a mirror and a warning, a line I had not crossed yet but was standing on. Under the shame a small awareness returned. The data was clear. The system was at failure load, and I was still alive to read it.

Anchor Card

Critical Load: *Mercy begins where structure ends.*

Principle: *Collapse is a forced pause that restores proportion.*

Protocol: *When systems fail, don't rebuild instantly, read what broke in sequence.*

Proof: The *sheriff's quiet restraint revealed order through mercy, not control.*

Observation logged

Pattern detected

Chapter 5

The Pattern Seen

Telemetry and confession

Telemetry Review

The morning after the sheriff left, the silence was not peace, it was pressure released from a failing system. The air felt heavy. The house felt hollow. Every dent, crack, and splinter looked like data. That is how my brain works, it cannot help but analyze. Even in the aftermath I was cataloging the damage like after a failed test, identifying points of failure, measuring impact, running the chain of causes. There is a moment after a catastrophic event when you do not feel guilt yet, only awareness. That was me, standing in my own wreckage, seeing my life as telemetry instead of tragedy. The front door was a structural breach. The holes in the wall were stress fractures. My wife and kids hiding from me was a system evacuation. Me still standing was a critical malfunction that somehow did not complete the failure sequence. I had seen this pattern before at work. When you push a rocket past tolerance and it does not explode, you do not celebrate, you study why, because if you do not it will happen again and next time it will not stop at cracks. That is what the sheriff's visit was, a nonfatal test fire, a warning before the full collapse, a miracle dressed as a system alarm. For the first time I was not blaming anyone else. Not my wife. Not my past. Not my father. The problem was internal. The variable was me. I could trace it back, every escalation, every blackout, every time I chose anger over truth. It was not random. It was a feedback loop, a signal bouncing around inside me with no ground path to release. That is when I realized something that changed everything, the same way a rocket fails for predictable reasons, so does a man. Sin, addiction, pride, violence are not mysteries. They are physics. Energy never disappears, it transfers. Pain from childhood becomes anger. Anger becomes control. Control becomes isolation. Isolation becomes the perfect environment for decay. Entropy always wins unless something external intervenes. That night the external factor was mercy, grace disguised as law enforcement, love disguised as restraint. Grace does not fix the system for you. It buys time to rebuild it. That morning I saw my entire life as data, every arrest, every broken thing, every moment of chaos, all pointing to a single truth, nothing breaks for no reason. If I could find the pattern, maybe I could find the design. The thought hit like a download, sudden and electric. I was not thinking about God yet, not consciously, but I could feel something watching, not judging, only recording, like a black box in the corner of every room collecting every decision, every word, every failure, waiting for me to stop flying blind long enough to listen. That was the first time I understood the Observer Effect as life, not physics. Observation changes the outcome, and for the first time I was watching myself instead of living on autopilot. The data was ugly, but it was truth, and truth, however brutal, is the first form of grace.

The Filter

Once I started viewing my life like data I could not stop seeing patterns, not just in what broke, but in how it broke. There was order in destruction, a consistency to the chaos, like something intelligent was behind it, not benevolent, but precise. It felt like a filter. I did not have language for it yet, but that is what it was. Every time I chose to drink, to lie, to lash out, something was taking notes. Not fate. Not karma. Something older, smarter, patient. It was not only me fighting myself. It was as if a system was running in the background of reality testing every input. What survives moves forward. What fails gets recycled. That is how filters work in engines, in machines, in souls. They catch debris that cannot pass through. In my childhood it was already there, the same pattern repeating, each trauma a data point, each temptation a calibration, each collapse a diagnostic. Temptation is not only an obstacle. It is a test. Evil is not random. It is targeted. The demonic is not creative, it is efficient. It studies you, knows your lineage, your triggers, your weak frequencies. It does not need to break you outright, it only needs to tune you slightly off resonance so your own system destroys itself. That is addiction as demonic resonance, an energetic hijack that starts with agreement. It cannot force you, but it can influence you, and if you open the door even a crack it enters, feeds, and grows. The alcohol was not only alcohol anymore. It was circuitry. Each drink a signal. Each blackout a blackout in more ways than one. Behind it all was that quiet intelligence, the filter. Scripture calls Satan the accuser, and in practice he operates like quality control. He does not create sin, he exposes it. He does not need to fabricate lies, he amplifies what is already in you. That is how you tell divine from demonic. God refines through love. Satan tests through temptation. When you fail you are not only punished, you are measured, not by God, but by the laws He built. Physics and faith do not contradict. You cannot cheat gravity. You cannot cheat entropy. You cannot cheat spiritual law. You either resonate with truth or you burn in distortion. Looking back I realized Satan had always been nearby, not with horns and smoke, only subtle interference, a thought, a feeling, a whisper that sounded like my own voice. That is the terrifying part. Demons do not need to shout. They need agreement. They operate like parasitic energy feeding on impulse, shame, and comfort. They do not always cause the storm, sometimes they keep you standing in it. The filter is not punishment. It is exposure. Every time I gave in it was not proof God abandoned me, it was proof I still had something worth testing. God did not send the devil to destroy me. He allowed him to reveal me. In that revelation the data made sense, even corruption needs order to exist, which means evil is backhanded evidence of design. Fear began to shift into comprehension. Pain became information. Chaos started speaking calibration. You cannot escape the filter, but you can pass through it.

Boundaries of Love

Once you see the filter you see it everywhere, not only in addiction and temptation, but in people, in systems, in authority. That realization hit hardest in the quiet after the sheriff left. I thought about who had power in my life and how they used it. Some protected. Some controlled. Some destroyed. For most of my life rules felt like chains, probation, restraining orders, curfews, authority that talked at me instead of to me. All authority looked like control, so I pushed back, rebelled, resisted. That night did not feel like control. It felt like a boundary, firm and unflinching, protective rather than oppressive. That is the difference I was never taught. Boundaries are not control. Control seeks to dominate. Boundaries exist to protect. Discernment lives there. The same intuition God gave me to feel the difference between temptation and conviction began to show the difference between true authority and counterfeit authority. I saw it in churches that preached fear instead of love, in leaders who used God's name to justify manipulation, in friends who wanted access without accountability, and in myself every time I used anger to get obedience instead of understanding. It shocked me to realize I had been mimicking what I hated. I had become controlling, not with rules, but with volatility. True authority does not intimidate and does not break people to prove it is real. True authority sets a line because it loves what is on the other side. That is what Stacie did that night. That is what the sheriff did. Neither excused me or condoned me. They drew a line and said, this far, no further. That is what God does. The commandments are not shackles. They are guardrails to keep you from falling off a cliff you cannot see in the dark. Satan flips it, selling control disguised as freedom, no rules, do what you want. It is a trap. Every boundary you cross feeds him. Every indulgence strengthens the parasite. Every freedom turns into a chain. God invites you inside His lines. On the surface it looks like restriction. Inside it is safety and life. It took decades to see that, and I am still learning. That was the start of a new paradigm, boundaries are love, not control, and if I wanted to rebuild my life I had to draw lines the way God does, not to punish, but to protect. The shift did not make me perfect or sober overnight. It gave me a lens. Once you have the lens you cannot unsee it. You begin to see where control masquerades as care, where love demands structure, where authority becomes service rather than domination. For the first time I believed I could live inside boundaries without feeling caged. Maybe the problem was not the line. Maybe it was my fear of it.

Hidden Code of Reality

Seeing the difference between control and boundaries revealed another pattern. It was subtle at first, then everywhere. Nothing was random. Not the way temptation hit. Not the timing of mercy. Not the build and release of chaos. It felt structured, as if code ran under the surface and I had been living inside it without knowing. I felt this as a kid watching people move in loops like NPCs. Back then it was intuition. After mercy and boundaries and filters it felt like confirmation. The chaos was not random. The mercy was not random. The test was not random. They were data points on a map. Even demons fit. They are not free agents. They operate like code, predictable, patterned, efficient. They do not invent new sins. They recycle old ones. They do not force. They influence. Always the same mechanisms tuned to different hosts. Step back far enough and it looks less like warfare and more like architecture, a system designed to reveal what is real, a simulation with moral gravity built in. Every choice has weight. Every action makes ripples. Every indulgence compounds. Physics calls it cause and effect. Theology calls it sowing and reaping. Engineering calls it feedback. Different languages, same law. Once you see it you stop believing in luck and coincidences and start believing in calibration. It is like a motherboard. To the untrained eye it is wires and chips. To an engineer it is elegant order. Every line goes somewhere. Every node has a purpose. Nothing is wasted. That is how my life began to look. A mess at first glance, a map if you look deeper. God was not passively watching. He embedded the code and left fingerprints in every loop, every test, every act of grace. I did not have the full language yet, but this was the seed of my thesis. Chaos leaves data. Read the data. Find the design. It is not about ignoring demons or romanticizing pain. It is about understanding that even the worst things, once exposed, reveal the pattern. Every temptation becomes a trace route. Every failure becomes a test log. Every act of mercy becomes a checksum that proves an underlying design. I was not out of the pit yet, but for the first time I had a compass. It did not point to self help. It pointed to something older and hidden in plain sight, the code of reality. Seeing the pattern did not make the pain vanish, but it changed its meaning. For the first time I saw symmetry inside the chaos. The same cycles that once felt like punishment now read like instructions. Every scar marked a place where a lesson had been welded in. It was not random. It was rhythm. The design was alive underneath it all, steady and patient. For a moment the weight lifted and I could breathe. The data was not condemning me anymore. It was guiding me. Maybe this was what grace actually looked like, not escape from consequence but the chance to understand it.

Anchor Card

Telemetry Review: *Data is confession without defense.*

Principle: *Honesty converts chaos into pattern.*

Protocol: *Review events as readouts, not accusations.*

Proof: *Every fracture plotted the same curve, grace formed the equation.*

Observation logged

Chapter 6

Entropy and Order

Decay reveals design

The Law of Decay

The day after the fracture my water heater started leaking and bled a slow scalding line down the tank. No drama, just drip drip, scale in the seat, pressure building, the system whispering. I kept mopping instead of fixing. That is how sin works, you get good at towels instead of turning the wrench. Entropy does not announce itself. It creeps in quietly, one molecule at a time, one compromise at a time. In physics it is the Second Law of Thermodynamics, every closed system moves toward disorder. Energy leaks. Heat dissipates. Structure decays. Left alone everything collapses. It is not just science, it is life. Addiction taught me that before any textbook did. When I drank, it was not chaos all at once, it was order dissolving slowly, my routines, my relationships, my body. Entropy disguised as pleasure. Each drink felt like control but it was decay. Sin works the same way. It does not crash the door. It seeps. It whispers. It starts with one compromise, one little it is not that bad, then another, and another, until you are no longer in control, the system is. The moment you stop inputting order, prayer, discipline, humility, gratitude, then that's when entropy begins. The system does not care about your excuses. The law just runs. That is why addiction feels inevitable. You cannot negotiate with entropy. You can only counter it with energy, divine energy. When you sin, you lose spiritual voltage. You leak power. You can feel it, that dull heaviness after giving in, that hollow exhaustion after anger or lust. You just burned fuel with no regeneration cycle. The paradox is that sin feels like energy in the moment, the hit, the rush, the escape, but it is counterfeit energy, pulling from reserves instead of renewal, charging you temporarily while draining the source over time. That is why Scripture calls sin death. It is not punishment, it is physics, a law of decay baked into the design. If you disconnect from the Source your system fails. Entropy does not stop because you pray harder. It stops when you reconnect. That is what grace really is, not magic, not a reset button, but divine reenergization. Grace reverses entropy by reintroducing God's energy into the system. For years I thought my drinking was rebellion. Now I know it was disconnection. My spiritual current was cut and the system compensated by burning whatever fuel it could, adrenaline, resentment, alcohol, pride. The byproduct was heat, waste, decay. I saw it in Texas everywhere. The canal by my property line grew algae when the level was low. Tools rusted in a week if I did not wipe them down. The truck battery sagged when I left the dome light on. The same laws govern combustion and the human soul. Burn too hot for too long without replenishment and you melt the structure that was meant to lift you. Yet even entropy has purpose. Without decay you never learn to calibrate. Without pain you never learn to realign. Decay reveals what needs repair. Sin reveals where you are disconnected. Entropy is the universe reminding you that you cannot sustain yourself. Once you see it that way, everything changes. The guilt fades. The shame loses power. You stop asking why am I broken and you start asking where am I leaking. The leak is the clue, the data point, the map back to God. The morning I finally fixed the water heater I could hear the relief in the pipes, the steady low rumble returning, and I knew that sound in my chest too. God was not asking me to be a hero. He was asking me to stop mopping and turn the wrench.

Resistance and Calibration

Every engineer knows you cannot stop entropy, but you can slow it, you can resist it, you can design around it, and if you are smart you can turn it into information. That is what grace is, resistance through recalibration, not denial of decay but the intelligent application of divine order against it. I used to think grace meant forgiveness, a cosmic hall pass. God knows your heart, as if that erased the damage. Grace does not ignore the data. Grace corrects it. In engineering you calibrate systems with resistance. You push current through, measure deviation, adjust until the signal stabilizes. Grace works the same way. It does not cancel the law of decay. It compensates for it. Where sin drains, grace replenishes.

Where entropy spreads, grace introduces new order. But the calibration is not passive. You have to cooperate with it. You cannot pray for calibration while pouring poison into your system. You must hold still long enough for the system to measure you. That was the hardest part for me, staying still while God adjusted me. Resistance began with small choices. No drink tonight. No lashing out when I felt the spark in my chest. No running when shame told me to disappear. Each no was an act of resistance. Each act became a calibration point. Each calibration made the next one slightly easier. It is the same in mechanics. The first adjustment feels violent. Bolts screech. Threads grind. Systems fight back. Then alignment clicks and everything flows. Noise drops. Efficiency spikes. That is how spiritual calibration feels. Painful at first because sin has warped you out of tolerance. When the Spirit tightens you into true alignment you start to hum again, in tune with the design. That is why suffering can be mercy. It is the wrench turning. It is the gauge reading the offset. It is God saying you are still fixable but this will hurt. I used to see my pain as punishment. Now I see it as measurement. Calibration is never cruel. It is precise. It happens because something still matters enough to be corrected. The same way I would pressure test an actuator until it held, God tested me until my faith held under load, not to break me but to prove I could bear weight. Resistance is faith in action. Faith is not a feeling. It is a feedback loop, the willingness to stand in pressure and trust the process of alignment. Grace makes that process survivable. Without it resistance burns you out. With it resistance refines you. Entropy still runs. Decay still whispers. Calibration restores balance so you stop swinging between chaos and collapse and begin operating within tolerance, not perfect, precise enough to keep moving. That is the secret most people miss. Grace does not excuse the system's laws. It fulfills them. It is divine engineering. Every time I resisted destruction and recalibrated even slightly I was running God's algorithm. Entropy fought to take me apart. Grace fought to hold me together. The only thing between them was my willingness to stay still long enough for God to tighten the bolts. Calibration log kept on my phone, three dials, Sleep, Food, Spirit. If two dials are red, no alcohol, no arguments, no decisions. When I honored that stupid simple rule entropy lost most of its free wins. On days I slipped I could feel the old frequency return, the short temper, the shallow breath, the restless eyes. On days I stayed inside the rule I had enough margin to pick up the guitar for ten minutes and play something, and even that small clean pattern told my nervous system this is the cadence, follow it.

Grounded Current

Electricity is simple when you strip it down. Charge builds. Energy flows. Resistance shapes the path. Everything from light bulbs to rocket systems needs one essential thing, a ground. Without it circuits fry. Current backs up. Voltage spikes. Wires overheat. The system burns itself out from the inside. That is sin, not superstition, not metaphor, a literal state of being ungrounded. Sin is charge without release, energy trapped and cycling through pride, anger, lust, envy, every current running wild with nowhere to go. The human soul was not designed to hold that much voltage alone. It was meant to flow through God, grounded in Him and regulated by His order. When you disconnect from that ground everything in your system reacts. Thoughts spark in loops. Emotions overheat. Addictions form like short circuits, desperate attempts to discharge the pressure somewhere, anywhere. Alcohol was a false ground for me. Every drink bled off tension for a moment but did not resolve anything. It was like connecting a live wire to metal instead of earth. You hear the sizzle, smell the smoke, think the danger has passed, but all you did was char the insulation. The current still hunts for home. I did not understand it then, but I was an open circuit. I kept generating current, ambition, obsession, anger, guilt, with nowhere for it to go. Every emotion stored instead of released became heat. Every failure I refused to face became resistance. Every moment I ran from God built static in my soul. Eventually I reached critical charge, the night of the fracture. The blackout was not only drunken chaos. It was system failure. Every alarm ignored, every warning light dimmed, the surge tearing through everything, my house, my family, my body. The damage was not random. It was electrical. Yet even in that short circuit something impossible happened. The system did not die. The breaker tripped. Mercy cut the power just long enough to save what was left. That was grace. Not words or rituals, literal intervention, a divine circuit breaker stopping a complete meltdown. After that I stopped seeing God as a distant judge and started seeing Him as the power grid that holds the universe. We are all wired into Him. Every act of obedience reconnects us. Every act of rebellion severs us. Every moment of repentance re establishes contact. That is why forgiveness is not only emotional relief. It is electrical grounding. It discharges the buildup. It resets voltage. It prevents overload. Without it the system cannot stabilize. Faith is maintaining that connection. Prayer is recalibration. Obedience is current flow. Gratitude is voltage regulation. Salvation is not escape from entropy. It is permanent grounding in infinite energy, a system that does not burn out because it is finally connected to its source. Once I understood that, everything else made sense, physics, sin, suffering, demons, deliverance. It was all circuitry, all code, one continuous design. Entropy was not the enemy. Isolation was. The leak was not the fatal thing. Disconnection was. The repair was not mystical. It was mechanical. Plug back in. Stay grounded. Let current flow. That is grace, not forgiveness you earn but current you receive. Once you are grounded you stop burning yourself out trying to be the power source. You stop playing God and let Him do His job, and that is when the lights come back on. The air was still but alive. The hum in the distance blended with the sound of my own breathing until I could not tell where one ended and the other began. The pulse of the world had slowed to match my own. For the first time in years, I was not trying to change the signal. I was listening. The wind moved through the trees like static that had finally found its frequency. Nothing extraordinary happened. Nothing needed to. That quiet was its own proof that the system could hold. I sat there until the sound of the earth became prayer and realized that peace was not silence. It was signal.

Anchor Card

Law of Decay: *Disorder is design revealing weak joints.*

Principle: *Entropy measures distance from truth.*

Protocol: *Trace leaks, repair proportion, restore grounding.*

Proof: *Forgiveness re-established current where bitterness had shorted the circuit.*

Observation logged

Chapter 7

The Observer Effect

Awareness changes outcome

Observer and Observed

From the beginning I was more of a witness than a participant. Even as a boy in Moreno Valley I stood at the edge of chaos watching everyone else spin. It was instinct at first, then survival, then design. I saw how people moved, how violence brewed, how one small motion could shift the energy in a room. Years later, standing in a SpaceX test bay, I learned the formal name for what I had been living since childhood. The observer effect. In the lab the rule is simple. The act of measurement changes what is measured. You cannot record pressure without affecting temperature. You cannot watch a particle without moving it. I understood that before I could spell it. Observation changes the observed. I used to think physics and faith were opposites, one made of data and the other of dreams. But the longer I studied both, the more they began to blur together. Maybe God was the first engineer, the one who measured everything in mercy. Every law and constant behaves as if someone designed it to be seen. Observation is not just awareness, it is communion. When you really see something, you become part of its existence. Maybe that is why prayer works. Maybe attention itself is sacred, because focus is the meeting point between the measurable and the divine. One night in composites test I made what felt like a small adjustment. I moved a strain gauge twelve millimeters to clean up a data set. On paper the component passed. On teardown it failed. The measurement itself had changed the load path. Observation faked the pass. It haunted me. How many times in life had I done the same thing and angled the gauge just enough to get the reading I wanted? How often had I measured myself in half truths to feel stable? The answer was every day. At first it kept me alive. Detachment was armor. In Moreno Valley it protected me from the chaos around me. At SpaceX it kept me steady when everyone else cracked under pressure. But detachment has a cost. You start thinking neutrality is safety. You start believing you can watch without being changed. For years that illusion worked. I became the calm eye in the hurricane, the one who never lost control, the one who could watch collapse and still hold the wrench steady. But entropy does not care about control. It only waits. Back in August 2023, in South Texas, the cracks had started. My performance looked flawless, but my internal readings were drifting. Alcohol became my calibration fluid. A drink at night to unwind. Then another to forget. Then the bottle as part of the routine. I told myself it was balance, stress relief, recovery. I told myself I was still functioning. And I was, but the readings were wrong. I was editing the data again. Every night I measured the system from a biased angle, and the truth kept slipping further out of frame. I was still producing results, still the guy who finished what others abandoned, still the one managers trusted with hardware worth millions. No one saw the static building underneath the surface because I did not want them to. Observation, I learned, is not just a tool, it is a weapon. What you choose to measure becomes what you feed. I had spent my life analyzing the world around me, but I refused to measure the decay inside myself. The result was predictable. My body fatigued, my patience thinned, my temper sharpened. By late 2024 the feedback loop had turned negative. I was living two lives. The precise launch and test operations specialist by day, the quiet addict by night. SpaceX rewarded my output, not my health. Every successful launch or test bought me another excuse to ignore the data. I had built an identity around performance so airtight that no one questioned how much of it was running on fumes. When January 2025 came, the system finally showed its first public failure. I was called and told the sentence no high performer ever thinks he will hear: "You are done." The firing was professional on the surface, surgical even, but to me it felt like a spiritual eviction. I had built my identity in that hangar, and in one hour it was stripped clean. I walked out with a badge deactivated at the gate, and a silence I had not felt in years. That was the real observer effect, when the system stops validating you, you are forced to observe yourself without the buffer of output. It is the kind of mirror that does not lie. I remember sitting in my truck afterward, staring at the plant across the street, the way the heat shimmered off the asphalt. My hands trembled against the steering wheel. My mind kept looping through the same phrase, "what now." After that I went home and told myself I would rebuild, that I would rest, that I would finally fix what was wrong. Instead, I watched the readings fall flat. Sleep gone. Prayer mechanical. Hope dull. I thought observation was neutrality, but it had become paralysis. You cannot watch entropy without feeding it unless you act. I did not act. By July 2025 the readings spiked. Pressure rose, isolation deepened, and the system finally failed in South Texas. That was the collapse, the fracture, the night mercy walked in wearing a badge. I survived the explosion, but not unchanged. That is when I finally understood the deeper law behind the observer effect. It does not stop at physics. Every system in existence changes under the gaze of truth. You cannot watch your own life without transforming it. You cannot face your sin without it starting to lose power. Observation is the beginning of redemption. Blindness keeps the demons fed. Seeing starves them. The moment I started watching myself with the same honesty I gave my launch pad or test stand the chaos began to unravel. Not instantly, not cleanly, but enough to know that truth itself was the first form of grace.

Faith as Measurement

Faith came later, not as religion but as data. After the fracture, when the alcohol left my system and the static quieted, I realized that faith was not something you feel. It is something you measure. Faith is believing without evidence, so I began treating it like calibration. Each morning I checked my pulse, slowed my breath, whispered a one line prayer, "Align my aim, not my outcome." Ninety seconds later I felt the difference. The day moved smoother, less friction, less static. Faith, I learned, was not blind. It was empirical. It had outputs. In quantum mechanics, particles behave as if they exist in several probable states until measured. In life, awareness works the same way, it turns potential into focus. That is what prayer does metaphorically. It collapses inner chaos into order by focusing belief. You move a possibility from theory into reality through attention. It is not control. It is participation in a system designed to respond to awareness. I tested it. I prayed not to avoid failure but to see it accurately. I prayed for clarity, not comfort. And clarity came, often brutally. I started noticing how my thoughts changed the outcome before the outcome changed the data. I began to see how every focus of attention carried energy. When I stared at guilt, the guilt grew. When I stared at grace, the guilt faded. Observation itself was force. Demons understand that principle better than we do. They are masters of focus manipulation. They feed on fixation and force your attention on the wrong frequency. That is why temptation works. It is not always about the act, it is about the gaze. The more you stare at the thing you should not touch, the stronger its gravity becomes. That is how they redirect current. They do not need to create new energy, they only need to steal your focus. Once I realized that, I began to weaponize observation against them. I named every dark thought out loud. I spoke every shameful urge into light. The moment something is seen, it loses half its power. Faith became my instrument panel. Prayer was like calibration. Gratitude felt like voltage regulation. Obedience guided current flow. When I aligned those dials, the readings stabilized. I learned that faith does not cancel the laws of physics, it mirrors their order in human life. The system of life was built to respond to attention. When you measure in truth, you alter the result. When you measure in fear, you distort it. The more I practiced this, the more I noticed something else. Faith and physics shared a parent. Both required discipline. Both punished denial. Both rewarded precision. Faith measures the unseen the way instruments measure heat you cannot feel. When you believe, you are not closing your eyes, you are opening another kind of sensor. By the time I hit my first month of sobriety, I could read my own spiritual telemetry the same way I used to read pressure graphs. I could see spikes of pride, dips of gratitude, short circuits of fear. And just like in test, every pattern told a story. The difference now was that I did not edit the data. I faced it. I let faith do what measurement does best, reveal truth. It was not religion that saved me, it was repetition. Every morning was calibration. Every night was review. Faith, when practiced like science, became structure. It gave the same satisfaction as running a perfect test sequence, only now the output was peace instead of performance. I stopped trying to force belief. I just kept showing up to measure it.

Hidden Observer

For most of my life I thought I was the one holding the clipboard. The scientist, the uneducated engineer, the detached analyst recording the chaos around me. I believed my precision made me safe. But the longer I watched, the more I sensed something watching me back. It started quietly. Late nights in the hangar, post run silence, just me and the hum of cooling metal. I would look at the telemetry screens and feel it. That same stillness I used to feel as a kid standing in the haunted house, only now it was not fear. It was awareness. For years I wore detachment like Boba Fett's armor. It was neutral, tactical, unshaken. Watching was how I survived. But at some point I realized that every time I observed, I was also being observed. God was there, not as an idea, but as a system presence. He had been logging my data since birth metaphorically, as though my life were a data log He could read. Every success, every blackout, every heartbeat was recorded. Every mercy cross referenced. Every silence marked as a pending response. I was not just living under law. I was living under measurement.

That realization dismantled the last of my arrogance. I was not the engineer controlling the test. I was the test. Every collapse was evidence. Every act of survival was data. Every prayer unanswered was a delayed calibration. The universe was not random. It was feedback written into form. The Hidden Observer was not watching to punish me. He was verifying His own equations, showing that grace holds even when the system fails. It made sense of everything I could not before. Why free will and sovereignty could coexist, why mercy followed wrath, why I was still alive after so many self inflicted implosions. I was not outside the experiment, I was its subject. God was not breaking me for entertainment. He was measuring me for endurance. After that, I stopped hiding the data. I stopped pretending I could fake clean readings. I started praying in real numbers "God, I am at thirty percent today. I am leaking. I am tired." I treated prayer like a report, not a performance. And I began to feel something shift. The same way a feedback loop stabilizes once the input matches the sensor, my soul began to level out. Being seen stopped feeling like exposure. It felt like belonging. For the first time I was not terrified of the gaze. I welcomed it. Because I finally knew what it meant. I was not being watched for failure. I was being studied for restoration. Every flaw mapped, every fracture noted, every repair prewritten into the design. That is the secret of the Hidden Observer. He is not waiting to grade you. He is waiting to calibrate you. And when I finally turned my eyes back toward Him, I realized He had never looked away. The observation was mutual. The experiment was grace itself.

Anchor Card

Measurement and Mercy: *Observation changes the observed.*

Principle: *Awareness stabilizes what it names.*

Protocol: *Speak the pattern aloud, presence collapses chaos into form.*

Proof: *Naming fear turned it measurable, ending its control.*

Observation logged

Chapter 8

Resonance

The frequency of grace

Destructive Interference

In physics, when two waves meet, they do not just pass
through each other, they combine. If their peaks align,
the energy amplifies. If their peaks and valleys oppose,
they cancel each other out. That is destructive
interference, and it was exactly what my life felt like
during that period. I had systems running everywhere,
work, home, fatherhood, faith. Each had its own rhythm.
Each had its own frequency." Frequency" here means
rhythm or emotional tone, not measurable hertz. Instead
of harmonizing, they were colliding. At SpaceX, I was
operating at a high vibration. Precision. Intensity. Flow. I
could work through exhaustion, strip systems down,
build them back up. My mind was at peak signal. I was in
sync with the machines, with the data, with the mission.
But at home, I was operating at a broken vibration.
Anger. Fatigue. Addiction. The same man who could set
up a launch pad for a rocket launch or a test stand primed
for a test and execute it precisely could not hold a dinner
conversation steady with his wife and son. I could
manage combustion, but not emotion. I could tame
pressure in steel, but not in flesh. And faith, faith was a
whisper under all that noise. Present but faint, like a

signal too weak to reach through interference. When those three waves collided, work, home, spirit, they did not amplify. They canceled. The peaks of one met the valleys of another, and the result was a life that looked stable from the outside but felt like static on the inside. From a distance, everything appeared functional. I had a respected job, a family, a home. But up close, every part of me was vibrating out of phase. I started noticing it everywhere. In the distance between me and Stacie when we spoke. In the way my son's eyes flicked away when I raised my voice. In the hollow echo of my own heartbeat at night, racing when it should have been resting. I would sit on the couch after work, Slack still pinging, my laptop open, the bottle gleaming in peripheral vision. Stacie would try to talk about bills, or plans, or how Kage was doing, but my mind was split between deadlines and dopamine. My answers came short, defensive, clipped. I told myself I was providing, that the grind was for them, that I could multitask life the way I multi tasked rockets. But every justification carried a frequency of its own, and it was destructive. Destructive interference does not just reduce energy, it erodes structure. When vibrations stay out of phase long enough, things break. Materials fatigue. Welds crack. Circuits fail. And people fracture quietly before they fall apart loudly. I could feel it happening in me. The late nights, the drinking, the arguments that started over nothing and ended in silence. They were not isolated failures. They were waveforms colliding beneath the surface, stress building invisibly in the joints. I told myself I was balancing it, but I was not. I was living at cross currents, one foot in precision, one foot in chaos, and the interference was eating me alive. Tuesday night, dinner on the stove, bottle winking from the counter. Stacie talking about something real, something that mattered, but my attention was split down the middle. Work peaked, home valleyed. Then I saw Kage sitting across the table, tense, shoulders tight, eyes flicking between us. I put the phone face down. Set a two minute timer. Two minutes of full attention shifted the table's vibration. The air changed. My son's shoulders dropped. Mine did too. It was the smallest thing, but it felt like something inside the system realigned. That was the first time I realized phase shifts were possible without blowing everything up. Little corrections prevent big fractures. I had been treating harmony like a miracle, something that just happens when life is good. But in that moment, I saw it for what it was, a discipline. Harmony is not born. It is tuned.

Harmonic Alignment

At SpaceX, the first thing I learned about resonance was that it is not just about force, it is about timing. You can have two systems made of the same material, built with the same precision, and one will still shake itself apart while the other holds steady. The difference is not strength, it is synchronization. That realization followed me home and would not leave. I started noticing how timing ruled everything. A few seconds of patience in a conversation could mean the difference between connection and conflict. One deep breath before answering could dissolve an argument before it started. Pausing before pouring a drink could feel like resisting gravity itself. It was not about perfection, it was about phase. A heartbeat off in a test could throw an entire data set into chaos. A heartbeat off in life could do the same. Resonance was not just physics, it was life. And alignment was not about doing more, it was about doing less out of sync. I did not quit drinking overnight. There was no cinematic moment of clarity, no voice from the sky, no sermon that fixed me. I just started paying attention. If I was angry, I did not explode, I studied it. If I wanted to drink, I did not pour, I timed the urge, watched it rise and fall like a waveform. If I felt disconnected from my family, I stopped pretending everything was fine and asked which frequency I was missing. Little by little, the noise thinned. I started catching moments, seconds really, where everything aligned. A day that ended without tension. A night when the bottle stayed closed and the house stayed calm. Every time it happened, I felt it physically, a hum beneath my ribs, subtle but real, like the vibration of a system settling into harmony. That is when I started seeing God differently, not as an untouchable ruler or a test I could fail, but as the tuning fork that all other frequencies calibrate to. When I matched my energy to His through honesty, patience, and humility, the static faded. The interference between my human noise and divine order started to soften. It was not serenity, not yet, but it was order. And order was enough. Resonance taught me something no equation ever had. You do not overcome chaos by silencing it. You overcome it by rising into better alignment, like a higher harmonic that steadies the system. The goal is not to control every frequency, it is to find the one that holds them all in tune. Maybe that is what faith really is, harmonic alignment between human signal and divine source. And the closer I tuned to it, the less effort it took to stay steady. There was a morning that summer when I sat outside before sunrise, drinking my smoothie, just listening. No noise, no alerts, no pressure. Birds starting to stir, the air still heavy with humidity. For the first time in a long time, the silence did not feel empty. It felt alive. The world was not waiting for me to fix it, it was already running, perfectly synchronized, with or without my interference. And I finally understood, alignment is not control. It is surrender.

The Frequency of Grace

After enough systems collapse, you stop asking why they failed and start asking what still holds. That is grace, the frequency that keeps vibrating even after everything else stops. I used to think grace was a feeling, a sigh after a storm, a fleeting peace you catch between chaos. I was wrong. Grace is not emotional. It is structural. It is the unseen resonance that holds you upright when every other signal drops out. It is what hums when you are too tired to speak and too ashamed to pray. There were nights before the fracture I wanted to stop, when I swore I would stop but did not, when I stared into the glass like it might hold an answer. But the bottle started tasting different, metallic, wrong, like feedback screaming through a speaker. My body flinched before my conscience caught up. That was not guilt. That was feedback. Grace was starting to reroute the current. I noticed it when I stopped talking long enough to hear my wife's silence without defensiveness. In faith, I noticed it when prayer was not a monologue anymore but a two way hum, energy flowing back and forth through the line. Grace has a sound in the heart. A quiet tone between chaos and control, as if it were resonance keeping structure intact. Every engineer knows when a system hums perfectly, you do not interfere, you let it run. That is how I began treating faith, not as something to fix or prove, but as something sacred that simply needed protection from interference. The more I protected it, the more it spread. Grace resonated like vibration through steel, one act of patience harmonizing into another, one moment of honesty echoing into forgiveness, one breath of gratitude syncing with the next. It was not dramatic. It was physics. Where sin distorts frequency, grace restores phase. Where pride amplifies noise, humility dampens it. Where chaos fragments, faith harmonizes. That was the revelation. Grace is not a miracle that defies nature. It feels like the law that completes it. Once I felt that, truly felt it, everything began to vibrate differently. The house. The air. Even my thoughts. It was as if the static finally cleared long enough for me to hear the signal that had been transmitting the entire time, steady, unwavering, alive. You are still here. You are still being tuned. Stay aligned. Grace, when it lands, does not feel like fireworks. It feels like a hum at idle that was not there yesterday. Same room. Same people. Same bills. Less rattle.

Anchor Card

Frequency of Grace: *Harmony proves alignment.*

Principle: *Truth vibrates at peace, deceit hums at tension.*

Protocol: *Audit tone before action, coherence outlasts force.*

Proof: *Forgiveness synchronized frequencies between heaven and human noise.*

Observation logged

Synthetic Resonance

Science eventually caught up to what the soul already knew, frequency changes everything. When two slightly different tones are played through headphones, one in each ear, the brain doesn't hear two sounds. It hears their difference and that difference becomes a pulse, a vibration that syncs neural rhythms. It's called binaural entrainment. Engineers use it to induce calm, focus, even sleep. It's measured in hertz, but it behaves like prayer. What fascinated me wasn't the science. It was the symmetry. Two conflicting frequencies meeting in one mind to create harmony. That's what grace does. That's what forgiveness does. They're emotional binaural beats, heaven's tone in one ear, human noise in the other. Maybe somewhere between them, your soul locks into peace. Its interesting how quickly my emotions changed with the rhythm. The frequencies could mimic meditation, fear, hunger, euphoria. It hit me that if man could manipulate emotion with sound, then faith was simply tuning the same instrument by divine hand instead of digital control. What you hear, consciously or not, is what you become. The brain doesn't argue with resonance, it obeys. That's why worship works. That's why lies spread. Every word, every rhythm, every vibration carries voltage that either syncs you toward coherence or drags you toward chaos. And once you realize that, you start guarding what you listen to. Not out of superstition, but out of system integrity. Because in the end, every sound is a signal. Some come from creation.

Some come from the code. Some come from the dark. Grace is the only one that stabilizes the frequency. That night the hum carried into the house. The lights were dim, dinner half done, the air still warm from the day. Stacie laughed at something Kage or Kolton said, and I found myself laughing too, not out of habit but because the sound fit. It felt like the entire room was tuned to one frequency again. No tension, no undercurrent, just rhythm. The television murmured from the other room while the ceiling fan clicked in slow time. Kage was talking about cars, about engines and sound, about how everything in motion sings its own note. I watched him speak. "The RTR package comes with an upgraded exhaust, aero package, and it broke records on the Nurburgring" he said. "What was the time?" I asked. "Six minutes and fifty two seconds" he replied. I took this moment in. He was right. Everything does. Even this. Even us. The years of chaos, the noise, the pain. They were still in the mix, but they no longer led the song. For the first time, peace was not silence. It was signal.

Chapter 9
Time Patterns and Design
Fractal law of redemption

Fractals of Life

I learned that failure is not chaos, it is repetition you have not mapped yet. Every cracked weld, every burned sensor, every unexpected vibration carries a fingerprint. Once you trace it you see the pattern, not as a single event but as part of a larger design repeating through time. Life worked the same way. I used to think I was trapped in cycles, addiction, anger, self-destruction. Over time I realized I was not looping in circles, I was spiraling, sometimes upward, sometimes down, always repeating the same geometry on a different scale. It was never the same event, just the same lesson refracted through a new lens. I remember one afternoon when Kage was younger, he was on the living-room floor surrounded by Lego pieces scattered like data points. He had built a spiral from mismatched plates, wide to narrow, vibrant colors, perfect curve. I knelt beside him. "Why did you build it like that?" I asked. He shrugged, eyes locked on the curve. "I just just put it together! See how it turns? It never really ends." I stared at it longer than I meant to. Something in the shape silenced the room. Stacie's voice broke the quiet first. "It's amazing how he sees patterns without even thinking about it." I nodded. "Some ratios are felt before they're named." Kage looked up at me, curious. That moment stayed with me. That is the nature of a fractal. Zoom in and it looks like chaos. Zoom out and it is perfect order. Every jagged line mirrors the whole. Every broken moment carries the blueprint of redemption. I began to see it everywhere, in relationships, in work, in faith. Every argument I repeated with Stacie was not random. It was the same unresolved pattern running on a tighter wavelength. Every relapse, every blackout, every whispered promise of I will never do it again was another rotation in the spiral. Each time I fell, I came down through the same geometry but with slightly clearer eyes. Beneath the repetition something was changing. Each loop brought more awareness, more precision. Each collapse revealed more of the structure. That is the paradox of the fractal. It teaches by collapsing. The pattern holds even when the shape shatters. When I first saw Fibonacci sequences in nature, they're amazing. You can see them in seashells, storms, and sometimes in galaxies, Curves of order hidden in chaos. The golden ratio wasn't just beauty, it symbolized consistency under pressure. Every curve, no matter how chaotic, obeyed the same constant. I began to wonder if pain worked that way too, if trauma was not punishment but recursion, grinding us slowly toward symmetry. Looking back the pattern was obvious. Birth, chaos, survival, clarity, collapse, rebirth, again and again, each stage an echo of the last but never identical. That is how God designs, through iteration. The divine does not erase chaos, He uses it. Entropy becomes the sculptor. Time becomes the chisel. The final shape, grace, emerges through repetition. The past keeps calling until you answer it. Lessons repeat until you learn them. Suffering feels circular but it is spiraling toward order. Creation itself is a fractal. Galaxies spiral the same way hurricanes do, the same way seashells do, the same way our lives do. A self-similar echo of divine intelligence repeating across every scale, from atom to soul. Every time I aligned even slightly closer to that rhythm, by forgiving, by surrendering, by trusting instead of forcing, I felt the pattern unfold one layer deeper. For the first time I was not afraid of the loops. I stopped calling them failures. I started seeing them as proof that God was still iterating me. I sat outside that night listening to the wind move through the trees and thought about how everything keeps cycling forward whether we notice or not. The same breeze that cooled the fields also touched the roofs and the wires, carrying a quiet order that never asked for credit. Maybe that is what grace really looks like when it settles. Not fireworks or visions, just continuity. The pulse that keeps the world breathing even when we forget to. I watched a plane climb through the clouds in the distance, its lights steady and small, and I felt a strange calm I could not explain. Maybe the world was never broken. Maybe it was just unfinished, still being refined in the same patient pattern that had been shaping me all along.

The Golden Ratio

Once I started seeing patterns I could not stop. Symmetry revealed itself everywhere, not in perfection but in proportion. The world was not built in straight lines. It curved and expanded in rhythm with one constant, the golden ratio. The same proportion that can be seen in the orbit of planets determines the reach of a fingertip. At first I called it coincidence. I believe it is God's fingerprint of design. My whole life I had been building against the ratio. Too much force. Too much control. Pushing when I should have balanced. Demanding symmetry where grace required curve. Every burnout, every argument, every collapse came from living outside proportion. God's design is not about control. It is about alignment. The ratio does not force balance. It reveals it. I started seeing it everywhere. When I gave too much of myself systems collapsed. When I withheld too much they starved. But when I found proportion between honesty and mercy, discipline and rest, strength and surrender, things stabilized. Even prayer changed. I stopped begging for outcomes and started calibrating for proportion. Not too much pride, not too little courage. Not too much planning, not too little faith. I began to tune myself to divine symmetry, the place where human effort meets God's grace in perfect proportion. Faith itself was a ratio, the balance between certainty and humility. Too much certainty becomes arrogance. Too much humility becomes paralysis. Held in proportion they create movement, grace in tension. Faith does not require perfection. It requires proportion. The ratio became a mirror for everything, my marriage, my leadership, the way I designed systems and raised my 2 sons. Every equation returned to the same truth. God designs through ratios, not rules. Perfect proportion, not rigidity, but resonance. Once I saw that I started looking at people differently. Every flaw and imbalance and wound was part of the curve that made them who they are. The goal is not to erase the imperfections. It is to align them within the larger pattern. Even scars can fall into symmetry. That is what grace does. It does not flatten you into uniformity. It brings your chaos into proportion with love. Launchpads and rockets and test-stand fixtures never survive by being perfect. They survive by proportion, mass to load, stiffness to damping, effort to rest. Every time I lived outside proportion something snapped. The same was true for me. When I pushed too hard, relationships fractured. When I had coasted too long, they drifted. But when I surrendered control and moved with rhythm instead of force I found harmony. That was when I realized God did not want perfection from me. He wanted proportion, the courage to live balanced between drive and peace, precision and surrender, order and grace.

Nonlinear Redemption

For most of my life I believed redemption was progress, a straight climb out of the pit, one step after another, leaving wreckage behind. But life does not move like that. Not in nature. Not in physics. Not in faith. Rockets do not rise in straight lines. They arc, bending gravity's will. Systems progress through feedback, through oscillation, through correction. Even light bends through gravity, curving around mass like a pilgrim tracing the edge of creation. Redemption works the same way. It is nonlinear. It does not erase failure. It integrates it. Every relapse, every heartbreak, every wrong turn becomes data, a variable in an equation too big to see from where you stand. For years I thought every collapse meant starting over. Now I know I was circling the same lesson from a higher orbit. Each return looked like failure but it was refinement, the same test, slightly harder, slightly closer to truth. Grace never skipped the math, It used it. When I first tried to quit drinking I treated it like a linear problem. If I stop, everything will improve. But the system was more complex. The addiction was not the cause. It was the output. The real variables were deeper like, pain, pride, exhaustion, emptiness. You do not debug a system by deleting the symptom. You trace the feedback. You watch the delay between cause and effect. You find the loop feeding the noise. That was where redemption began, not in stopping the output but in reprogramming the feedback. Replacing guilt with gratitude. Reframing failure as data. Tuning despair into awareness. Slowly the system stabilized. Not because I was perfect but because I accepted imperfection as part of the formula. In engineering that is called tolerance, the range within which something can deviate and still function. For the first time I gave myself a tolerance. In that grace I began to heal. I stopped expecting straight line improvement, no more "tomorrow I will be better." I watched for patterns instead. Was I moving in the same direction over time even if the path curved back on itself. Was I learning faster each time I fell. Were my mistakes smaller, my corrections quicker. Those became my metrics of redemption. With every pass through the loop I felt more calibrated. My reactions softened. My prayers shortened. My gratitude arrived sooner. That was how faith grew. Not by avoiding gravity but by learning to arc through it. Every spiral and setback and oscillation was shaping something stable inside me. A deeper resonance. A divine rhythm. The frequency of grace itself, steady and patient, humming through the noise. When I looked back from that vantage point I finally saw the pattern clearly. None of it was wasted. Not the drinking. Not the wreckage. Not the arrests. Not the pain. Every failure was a data point in God's equation. Every collapse was part of the fractal. Every loop, no matter how chaotic, curved toward order. Redemption was not escape. It was integration. And grace was not a second chance. It was the realization that I never left the pattern to begin with. The later relapses were getting further apart, until the last one. Nonlinear redemption looks uneventful from the outside. But from the inside it feels like orbit.

Anchor Card

Fractal Law: *Every scale repeats the lesson until proportion holds.*

Principle: *Micro failure reflects macro truth.*

Protocol: *Study recurrence, apply correction across dimensions.*

Proof: *The same curve shaped childhood and career, each revealing divine geometry.*

Observation logged

Pattern detected

Chapter 10

Simulation and Multiverse

Breaking the loop

NPC Loops

It started as a joke. I used to call people NPCs, non-player characters, like they're background figures stuck in their routines. The guy who complained about the same things every day, the coworker whose gossip loops never ended, the friend who always talked about changing but never did. It made me feel separate, awake in a world asleep. Over time the joke stopped being funny. The pattern was not about them. It was about me. People moved through their scripts, repeating the same arguments, the same excuses, the same fears dressed in new clothes. They were not living. They were executing. And the more I watched, the more I realized I was running the same code. Addiction made me an NPC in my own story. Every night I promised to stop. Every morning I failed. Every prayer recycled the same words. Every fight ended in silence. I could predict myself like clockwork. It wasn't rebellion. It was recursion. The worst part was realizing I wasn't deciding anymore. I was reacting. Somewhere along the line, choice had been replaced by programming. I had turned myself into background noise. I remembered reading about simulation theory years earlier. The idea that consciousness could exist inside a coded reality? This was different. Life wasn't fake. Sin was the glitch. Every lie, every indulgence, every act of denial rewrote the code. The more I repeated the same choices, the tighter the loop became. I was running a corrupted script. The Bible said it first, eyes open but they do not see, ears open but they do not hear. That was system language, not metaphor. Darkness doesn't need to possess you, it just needs you to stop paying attention. Demons don't drag you, they whisper at your weakest frequency. Fear when you feel unseen. Anger when you feel dismissed. Lust when you feel worthless. They don't force you off course, they lean just enough to keep the loop running. The worst prison isn't hell. It's autopilot. Awareness became my first act of rebellion. The moment you observe a pattern, it begins to lose power. That's physics and faith in the same breath. Observation changes the outcome. Truth, in that sense, is light. Light exposes code. Information rewrites it. One night in Texas I caught my reflection in the window. Drink in hand. Eyes empty. Words on repeat. "Tomorrow will be different." It never was. I stood there long enough to feel disgust crawl up my throat and whispered, "This is a loop." The words felt foreign, mechanical. I put the bottle down, watched it sit there like a test artifact, and said out loud, "Choice." The silence that followed was heavy but alive. Later, I tested it again. A gas station at midnight. A Tall Boy sweating under fluorescent light. Loop said, open, sip, disappear. Choice said, not tonight. I put it back and drove home. Nothing cinematic happened except the next morning existed. Sometimes the miracle is that simple. Survival isn't fireworks. It's exiting the loop.

Branching Paths

Seeing the loop was one thing. Seeing the map was another. The moment I woke up inside my own life, I realized every decision felt like a fork. Every action closed one possibility and opened another, like collapsing a quantum choice. Physics had hinted at it the whole time. Quantum theory says a particle exists in multiple states until observed. Observation collapses the wave into one outcome. It sounds abstract until you realize you are doing it every day. Every time you act or refuse to act, you collapse a possibility. Every reflex discards an alternate future. For most of my life I thought I was stuck on rails, born broken, die broken, one linear path from chaos to decay. But when I mapped my choices, I saw it differently. Every failure wasn't final. It was a fork. I hadn't been circling hell. I'd been choosing the same low branches over and over. That's when sovereignty and free will finally made sense. God's plan wasn't a single road. It was a network. Every path accounted for. Every detour mapped. Every missed turn recalculated. Grace was the reroute, but I still had to turn. Darkness worked the same system from the opposite side. It didn't block me. It biased me. One whisper, one distraction, one hit of dopamine in the moment of decision, and I'd pick the lower lane again. Once I saw it, I couldn't unsee it.

Awareness changed everything. I started testing the theory in small ways. A breath before answering Stacie. A prayer before reacting. A pause before the pour. I would ask, "Loop or choice?" That tiny act created space, and in that space, new timelines appeared. They weren't grand at first. Just small detours that led me toward peace instead of pressure. Then something strange started happening. Opportunities appeared that I hadn't earned. People arrived at the exact moment I needed them. Problems softened that had been immovable for years. It felt like quantum mechanics meeting grace in real time figuratively, not physical quantum events but spiritual cause and effect. Sin collapses potential. Faith restores it. Clicking "Apply" to SpaceX was one of those branches. Updating my resume on a night when I felt unworthy was another. Sovereignty wrote the map. My click chose the lane. Not long after that, I saw the same principle at work in my son. Kage had been frustrated with his younger brother, the kind that used to end with slammed doors and words we both regretted. But this time he stopped. He took a breath, got off his phone, and said, "I can't talk right now. I'll come back to it." The words were calm, matter of fact, no anger behind them. It caught me off guard. I just nodded and watched him walk away. He had done something I never could at his age. He broke the loop before it broke him. That night, when he came back, the problem was solved and the tension was gone. Watching him handle it with that kind of clarity felt like seeing the system evolve. It was grace in motion, proof that awareness multiplies once it takes root. I did not need to say anything. The loop was already rewritten. I didn't understand then how deeply the system ran. Every loop I broke wasn't just about me. It was generational. My choices were reprogramming the legacy my son would inherit. The code of my bloodline was being rewritten in real time. That realization was terrifying because it killed all excuses, but it was also liberating. My past didn't lock my future. One conscious act of faith could break loops that had run for generations. I saw it one night at the table with Kage, working on his a project. He drew orbits with colored pens, each one intersecting another, labeling the paths. "So if a planet moves even a little bit wrong, everything else changes, right?" he asked. I nodded. "Exactly. That's why small changes matter." He looked up at me. "So people are kind of like planets too?" I smiled. "Yeah, we are. Every choice pulls on the universe a little." He went back to messing with his project while I just sat there, staring at him, realizing the truth of it. That was grace. The map was still unfolding, but this time, I wasn't just watching it. I was steering.

Breaking the Loop

The first time I consciously broke a loop, it felt like heat leaving my body. For years, addiction had run as automatic code. Stress meant drink. Success meant drink. Loneliness meant drink. Input, output, repeat. I was a system without freedom. When I finally decided to test it,

I treated myself like an experiment. Observe, predict, interrupt. The trigger hit, the urge rose, and I whispered, "Loop or choice?" That simple phrase stalled the command line. The pause was small, but it was enough for grace to enter. Addiction thrives on speed. It hides in reflex. When you slow down, it starts to lose voltage. I prayed, not theatrically, not perfectly, just three words, "God, help me." The craving didn't vanish, but I could see the path ahead. The shame, the silence, the same morning-after apology. I could also see the alternative, a quiet victory, a night without collapse. That night I didn't drink. Nothing outside me changed. The bills were still there. The air was still heavy. Stacie was still distant. But something internal flipped. The output changed. Breaking loops never felt triumphant. It felt raw, shaky, human. But every act of resistance stretched the pause a little longer. Each pause made the code weaker. I began to use the same process for anger, lust, despair. Feel the surge. Stop. Ask. Pray. Choose. The results were subtle but undeniable. The reflexes slowed. The circuits rewired. That's when I finally understood what renewing the mind meant. It wasn't poetry. It was literal reprogramming. Each prayer formed a new path. Each pause rerouted the current. Over time, the old loops corroded. I built a simple rule for myself, three steps to override the script. One, touch my skin to feel something real. Two, inhale deep enough to smell the air, proof of presence. Three, name one positive truth to balance the negative. Sometimes it was, "I'm still here." Sometimes it was,

"God hasn't left me." By the time I cycled through the steps, the program had lost control. Weeks later, I noticed the cravings came later. Months later, they came quieter. Each loop broke like an old circuit burning out. Deliverance wasn't dramatic. It was slow rewiring. Darkness depends on automation. Awareness ruins automation. The moment you invite God into the pause, the system changes state. Awareness is divine interference. Grace is the patch. Faith is the new input. Every decision became data, every pause became a signal, every prayer became code repair. And over time, the loops fell apart. Relationships softened. My son's laughter came easier. Silence stopped sounding like punishment. For the first time, I felt conscious inside my own life. I was no longer background process. I was a participant in design. That's the secret written into everything I'd learned from rockets, from pain, from Scripture. Sin collapses possibility. Grace expands it. Observation activates choice. Choice invites God. That's how loops break. That's how freedom begins.

Anchor Card

Branching Paths: *Every choice collapses potential into path.*

Principle: *Awareness multiplies freedom, blindness narrows it.*

Protocol: *Choose consciously, observe consequence without denial.*

Proof: *The loops broke only when I accepted authorship of my own timeline.*

Observation logged

Chapter 11

The Human Filters

Signal integrity through temptation

Temptation as Test

Temptation used to feel like proof that I was broken. When it came, I took it as evidence that I was still unworthy, still corrupted, still too human to carry the kind of faith I claimed to have. Every relapse, every late-night urge, every spike of anger or lust felt like a divine reminder that I wasn't healed. But after years of watching the data, I began to see it differently. Temptation wasn't a punishment. It was a test signal. In engineering, you send pulses through a system to locate its weak points. You don't do it to destroy the circuit. You do it to reveal what needs reinforcement. Temptation works the same way. Every craving, every thought, every flicker of rebellion is a diagnostic pulse exposing where your system isn't yet grounded. That's what I began to see in my life. The tests weren't random. They were measured. Precision-engineered. When I was tempted to drink, it wasn't about alcohol, it was about control. When I was tempted to lash out, it wasn't about anger, it was about pride. When I was tempted to isolate, it wasn't about peace, it was about fear. Each signal revealed the same truth. I was still running old code, and on one night, a message landed in my inbox. Kind words, curiosity, an invitation laced with flattery. The voltage spiked. For a moment, the old self flickered to life, ready to rationalize, ready to drift. But this time I caught it. I spoke out loud, "Test signal." The word itself killed most of its power. Blocking killed the rest. I sat in silence, staring at the dark screen, realizing I'd just witnessed temptation in its purest form. Not a moral failure, but a functional test. I started to think about Satan differently. He wasn't some red demon lurking in shadows. He was more like a malicious engineer probing the system. He doesn't invent new weaknesses, he exposes the ones already present. He studies your blueprint, your lineage, your reactions. He doesn't guess. He observes. Then he sends the same temptation back at slightly different frequencies until he finds an opening. That's how he works. Not omniscient, but relentless, and God allows it. Not as cruelty but as calibration. Because resistance builds integrity. Without pressure, circuits remain untested. Without testing, there's no proof they can carry load. When I started treating temptation like telemetry instead of shame, everything changed. Instead of asking, "Why am I so weak?" I started asking, "What is this showing me?" The shame turned to strategy. Every time I identified the signal, the noise dropped. Every temptation became data. And once you have data, you can fix almost anything. I learned that even spiritual warfare obeys natural law. The enemy can't overpower divine design, he can only manipulate unused bandwidth. He can't force sin, he can only amplify desire. And when you start observing yourself with the same precision you used to analyze machines, temptation loses most of its voltage. It stops feeling like condemnation and starts feeling like calibration. It's not proof of failure. It's proof of what still needs grounding. That's what I realized the night I turned off the phone and walked back to bed. Stacie was already asleep. I stood there watching her breathe and felt it. The quiet after the test. Peace disguised as fatigue. I could breathe easy and rest knowing I did the right thing. I understood then what the test was really about, not proving strength but refining loyalty.

Signal Integrity

Every signal, no matter how pure, is worthless if it can't survive transmission. Every engineer knows that. You can generate perfect current at the source, but if your lines aren't shielded, interference will twist it beyond recognition. Human beings are built the same way. We are conductors of spirit and consciousness. Our thoughts, emotions, and actions are like electrical signals moving through biological and spiritual hardware. And just like any circuit, signal integrity determines whether that energy produces life or distortion. For years, my signal was chaos. I had power but no protection. I prayed when I was desperate and went silent when I felt strong. I'd study Scripture and then drown it out with noise. I'd try to love my family but transmit bitterness through every look and tone. I was a live wire with insulation stripped.

Every outside frequency like stress, temptation, resentment all jumped straight into my circuitry. It was no wonder I burned out. Once I started viewing life as a signal path, everything made sense. Prayer wasn't an obligation, it was grounding. Scripture wasn't just text, it was shielding. Fasting wasn't punishment, it was recalibration. Forgiveness wasn't weakness, it was clearing corrosion from the contact points. Even food and sleep mattered. My body was the physical interface of my spirit, the literal hardware through which all energy flowed. You can't expect divine signal to transmit clearly through poisoned wire. I stopped treating my body like a dumpster and started feeding it like equipment I planned to keep running at peak load. Sleep, clean food, water, magnesium before bed, protein before caffeine, Psalm before scroll. None of it was mystical. It was maintenance. The same way I would never run a static fire test with damaged hardware, I stopped running my life through unmaintained hardware. The effects were measurable. The static began to fade. I could sense interference before it hijacked thought. I could feel when something foreign was trying to inject itself into my signal. Dark influences feed on noise. They can't create energy, they can only distort focus. They amplify fear, blur truth, mimic familiarity. They don't destroy, they disorient. And disorientation is enough to crash a system if you let it. Shielding prevents that. I remember one night arguing with Stacie. It started small with tone, defensiveness, a misunderstood sentence and within seconds, voltage spiked. I felt the old pattern winding up, the one that used to end in shouting or slammed doors. But instead of firing back, I stepped outside barefoot and put my feet on the pavers. The air was hot and heavy, the night humming with insects. I whispered, "God, ground me." Within minutes, the charge dropped. I walked back in, looked her in the eyes, and apologized. That was new. That was system integrity holding under load. Over time, I started to recognize what clarity actually felt like. Peace that didn't depend on outcome, quiet that didn't feel empty, direction that didn't come from fear. The more I maintained that state, the more the world around me aligned. My conversations with Kage became easier. His guard started to drop. He laughed more. My thoughts sharpened. I wasn't operating on guesswork anymore. The signal was clean. Shielding wasn't about perfection. It was about staying tuned under pressure. Because even the purest source can't reach you if you let noise run the line. The more grounded I became, the more I realized that the voice of God isn't thunder. It's frequency. You don't hear it when you're loud. You hear it when you're still enough for the current to hum. Every time I stayed calm, it wasn't me. It was the system working. It was grace running its algorithm in real time, taking what would have been anger or panic and routing it somewhere safe. I could feel it sometimes, that quiet transfer of energy when something inside me wanted to fight but instead leveled out. That is not self control. That is divine architecture stabilizing a damaged circuit. My only job is to stay connected long enough for the correction to complete.

Emotional Frequencies

In recent years, they found something fascinating. Sound can steer emotion. Two tones, each fed into opposite ears, can create a third rhythm inside the brain. The body responds to heart rate, hormones, even hunger. It's called binaural entrainment, but it's more than technology. It's a good analogy for spiritual physics. Because the same way those frequencies can induce calm or chaos, temptation does the same thing to the soul. The enemy doesn't always speak. He broadcasts. He floods your environment with emotional frequencies, anger in news feeds, lust in entertainment, despair in silence, until your inner signal syncs to it. That's interference. It's not random, it's targeted. Demons use the same principle as audio engineers. Repetition, rhythm, resonance. They don't need possession when they can program you with pattern. That's why Scripture says "faith comes by hearing." Because everything you hear, everything you feed your senses, either tunes you closer to truth or further into distortion. I started testing it myself, not as ritual, but as experiment. Worship instead of white noise. Silence instead of scrolling. Gratitude whispered into the air before bed. These small gestures practiced over time felt like weight lifting off my shoulders. Like I could breathe again. My body changed. My patience stabilized.

The data was irrefutable. Attention determines alignment. We are tuning forks walking on two legs, vibrating between heaven and static. And whoever controls your focus controls your frequency. That's why guarding your ears and your mind isn't moralism, it's maintenance. The wrong frequencies can make you crave sin the same way the right ones can pull you toward grace. The system doesn't care where the input comes from, it only knows how to resonate. Faith is learning to filter the feed. Don't become a product of the environment. What goes in is one thing, but what comes out is is a different story.

Error Correction

Every system fails eventually. Heat builds. Data corrupts. Circuits drift from calibration. That's not design flaw, it's physics. That's why engineers build redundancy. A checksum, a feedback algorithm that compares what was sent to what was received and repairs the data before collapse. Grace is the divine checksum. The built-in self-healing protocol written into creation. I didn't understand that for most of my life. I thought grace was for people who couldn't handle consequences. I thought failure erased value. So I built a system that punished itself. When I made a mistake, I hid it. When I sinned, I drowned it. When I lost control, I pretended I hadn't. I was running without redundancy, so every fault was fatal. Until the night I couldn't hide anymore. After the fracture, after the sheriff, after everything I'd broken came into full view, I sat in silence trying to understand how I was still alive. My life had crashed, but somehow the system hadn't died. That's when I saw it. The data was still transmitting. If the system was still sending signal, the Designer hadn't abandoned it. Grace wasn't pity. It was process. It was God resending truth until I finally received it. That realization broke me open. Grace wasn't a one-time pardon. It was continuous error correction. Every time I failed, the system didn't erase me, it recalculated. Every time I lied, it sent me new opportunities to tell the truth. Every time I fell, it replayed the lesson until I learned to stand. It wasn't resetting the data, it was restoring the accuracy. That's why Scripture calls grace unfailing. Because it's built into the architecture. Demons hate that law. They feed on guilt because guilt convinces you the checksum failed. It convinces you your data can't be recovered. That's their lie. But as long as the Source remains connected, the checksum always runs. I built a real-world version of that protocol for myself. When I slipped, I didn't hide. I reported. "State, urge, next step." Three words. Ground, pray, execute. It wasn't confession for pity, it was correction for continuity. Stacie didn't need to fix me. My friends didn't need to advise me. Their only job was to mirror truth back until I realigned. It worked. The shame that once burned for days dissipated in hours. The static cleared. The signal returned. Grace had recalibrated me again. I began to notice something deeper. The process didn't just fix the error, it reinforced the structure. The more I failed and recovered, the stronger the circuit became. The tolerance widened. The system learned. I learned. God doesn't build for perfection. He builds for recovery. Entropy tests the system, but connection brings it home. That's the hidden mercy behind it all. Sin corrupts the signal. Grace resends it. Failure doesn't destroy you, it reveals where the design holds under stress. That's not weakness. That's divine engineering. Grace isn't a miracle that defies physics. It's the law that completes it. The checksum never stops running. The data never truly dies. And as long as I stay connected to the Source, I will always trend back toward order. Every relapse, every argument, every fall. It was all just noise waiting to be filtered. Every correction, every reconciliation, every quiet prayer. It was all part of the self-healing design. That's what grace really is. The constant recalibration of a soul learning to stay online through the static.

Anchor Card

Signal Integrity: *Temptation tests connection, not worth.*

Principle: *Interference exposes open ports of pride.*

Protocol: *Ground through confession, shield through gratitude.*

Proof: *Once interference was logged, clarity returned and peace stabilized.*

Observation logged

Chapter 12

Systems of Life

Closed-loop faith through adaptive control

Closed Loop Faith

The difference between chaos and design isn't perfection. It's feedback. A closed loop system monitors itself. It doesn't wait for catastrophic failure to make adjustments. That's what faith eventually became for me, not a belief, but a control system. For most of my life, I lived open loop. I reacted to stress, chased control, overcorrected, crashed, and called it progress. I mistook motion for growth and emotion for change. It was chaos disguised as evolution. I woke up swearing I'd do better, then fell into the same patterns because there was no calibration, no feedback. After the fracture, everything that wasn't true burned off. I stopped seeing faith as something you feel and started seeing it as something you run, a closed loop of awareness, correction, and grace. In engineering, feedback loops take the output, measure it, and feed it back into the input. That's how rockets stabilize, thousands of adjustments per second, too small to see but essential to flight. That's how your body keeps you upright. How your heart keeps time. How creation sustains itself. It's not perfection, it's constant micro correction. Faith works the same way. Prayer isn't proof of weakness, it's input correction. Reflection is data logging. Repentance is recalibration. Grace is the regulator that keeps the system from burning up under load. I used to think following God meant suppressing my instincts, muting my nature, pretending I was fixed. Now I see it means aligning the code, learning how He designed me, then feeding back my output through His truth instead of my own logic. It began small. I woke early, prayed for two minutes, and sat still long enough to hear silence. I ate instead of skipping meals and called it discipline, not indulgence. I wrote before I made a smoothie and treated that as calibration, not creativity. They weren't rituals, they were signal corrections. I was retraining my feedback loop, not perfection, just continuity. When I prayed, I didn't ask for miracles. I asked for alignment. When I sinned, I didn't promise perfection. I reported it like a fault log. "God, here's the data. Here's what failed." And then I adjusted. My blender became my control panel. Most mornings, I wrote one correction in my notes on my phone and would make my smoothie and review my notes. Speak slower. Listen first. Eat with Kage. Hug Stacie before leaving. Each note was a micro calibration in motion. It felt mechanical at first. Then it became natural. Like reprogramming muscle memory that had been wired wrong. Kage started noticing before I did. One morning he walked in and saw me reading one of them that said "Don't rush the morning." He grinned. "You gonna listen to your own rules today?" I smiled back and said, "That's the plan." He didn't know how much that moment meant.

Because that one sentence, that teasing, casual tone, was feedback. It meant my output was finally reaching him again. The signal wasn't lost. That's when I realized the same logic that builds rockets can rebuild a man. Both require feedback, calibration, and power from a stable source. Lose the source and entropy wins. Stay connected and order sustains itself. Faith stopped being a belief in God's existence. It became trust in His process. Not superstition, system logic. Not emotion, architecture. Every prayer was an adjustment. Every reflection was data. Every day I stayed in the loop, I drifted less. Every day I let the feedback guide me, I found a little more peace.

Redundancy and Mercy

If you've ever built a critical system, you know one rule. Single fault tolerance is deliberate. No engineer designs a rocket, an aircraft, or even a satellite without redundancy. You double the sensors. You triple the actuators. You create backup pathways so if one channel fails, another takes over. You design mercy into the mechanism. That's what God did with us. He didn't build us to live up to perfection. He built resilience. Every human is a network of redundancy. A body that heals. A mind that rewires. A spirit that regenerates through grace. When one fails, the others compensate. That's mercy, a backup circuit kicking in before collapse. I just never saw it that way before. Every relapse felt final. Every mistake, permanent. Every failure, a total loss. But looking back, the pattern was obvious. Every time I crashed, something intervened. A sheriff stepped between me and destruction. A stranger looked at me like I still had value. A brother drove across the country in a rental to pull me out of the wreckage. None of that was coincidence. That was redundancy. When my system failed, God rerouted the current through His own network until I could stand again. That's mercy in its purest form, grace through flesh and timing. I remember that night when my brother showed up. I hadn't called him. I hadn't called anyone. But he knew. He just knew. The knock on the door wasn't loud. It was steady. I opened it expecting a lecture. He didn't talk about faith or forgiveness or failure. Just stability. The silence between us wasn't judgment. It was signal transfer. God had routed mercy through him, bypassing my burned out system entirely. He didn't save me with words. He saved me with presence. That was the first time I understood what divine redundancy looks like up close. Mercy isn't a soft feeling. It's structural intelligence. It's the system rerouting current through alternate paths. Forgiveness isn't weakness, it's recovery code. You can blow a seal and still land. You can lose altitude and still survive. Because the structure was never relying on you alone. That's the genius of divine design. The backup system engages before the crash completes. Once I saw it, I stopped panicking when I felt weak. I stopped interpreting mercy as pity. Mercy is precision, a safety algorithm that triggers exactly when you can't handle the load. When I'm at the end of my capacity, I look for the reroute. The friend who texts, the verse that surfaces, the stranger who smiles when I don't deserve it. Those aren't coincidences. They're evidence that God still has me on the network. I used to think grace was a one way current flowing from heaven down. Now I see it's distributed. It runs through people, through timing, through love that feels random but isn't. I've been caught by that network more times than I can count. And every time I am, I realize the truth. The system was never built to fail without recovery. God didn't design us to run solo. He designed us to run redundant.

Adaptive Control

Every stable system eventually meets a condition it wasn't built for. The load increases. The pressure shifts. The code written for yesterday no longer fits today. That's when feedback alone isn't enough. You can't just correct. You have to adapt. In engineering, that's adaptive control, when the system learns its environment, adjusts parameters in real time, and maintains stability under changing conditions. Faith works the same way. Rigid belief cracks under turbulence. Living faith flexes. For years, I treated faith like static code, Pray, obey, repeat. That worked when life was predictable. But when storms came, it failed. Because life isn't static. It evolves mid flight. The environment changes, and the code has to evolve with it. When I finally began treating faith as adaptive control, everything clicked. Prayer wasn't just communication, it was recalibration. Scripture wasn't a list of rules, it was stored data from those who'd learned the algorithm before me. Grace wasn't a patch, it was an auto tuning process written into the soul. I remember sitting at the kitchen table after losing my job at SpaceX. My heart was hammering, my mind in loops, my hands shaking as if the adrenaline hadn't stopped from months earlier. I prayed, but it didn't feel like prayer. It felt like troubleshooting. "God, what do I adjust?" The answer didn't come as words. It came as stillness, an instinct to stop forcing clarity and just observe the system. That was adaptive control. My faith was learning new parameters. My pride was losing priority. My system was tuning itself to conditions it hadn't faced before. Even sobriety required adaptive faith. The stress spikes came in new forms, not the chaos of rockets or arrests, but the slow corrosion of boredom and silence. That's when I learned to run my sequence. Pause. Pray. Observe. Adjust. "PPoA." Simple and stupid. It worked every time. When stress rose, I'd breathe and say it out loud. Pause. Pray. Observe. Adjust. By the time I reached the fourth step, the voltage dropped. The loop broke. The craving passed. God doesn't need eloquence. He just needs input. That's when I understood what relationship with Him really was. It was not religion, not repetition, but continuous adaptive communication. He sends new data. I respond. I drift. He recalibrates. I fail. He adjusts. Over and over, until chaos becomes coherence. It's not perfection. It's process. Even sanctification is adaptive control. You don't wake up holy. You tune, adjust, recover. Every act of humility, every moment of surrender, every correction through grace, all real time adaptation between Creator and creation. That's why He built prayer, fasting, and gratitude into us. They're not rituals, they're input methods. Stability protocols for the human soul. Some days I still crash. Some days I still burn more fuel than I should. But I don't spiral anymore. I look at the system, read the data, and adjust. Because now I understand the purpose of turbulence. It's not punishment. It's calibration. The universe itself works that way. God didn't create a perfect machine. He created an adaptive one. We weren't designed to be flawless. We were designed to be responsive, capable of course correction through connection. That's what faith really is. Not blind obedience, but real time collaboration with the mind that designed you. Every failure, every prayer, every quiet moment of awareness is the same process repeating. Feedback, correction, refinement, grace. A living circuit between creation and Creator, adjusting endlessly until order overcomes entropy. That night the house was quiet except for the soft creak of the ceiling fan and the footsteps of my kids moving around the kitchen. No chaos, no sharp tones, just the rhythm of normal life finally holding steady. Kids were fed and in bed, house was clean, dogs were calm. The system had stabilized. Peace wasn't silence anymore. It was signal. It was the sound of life running as it was designed to. For years I chased control and called it faith, but standing there in that ordinary moment, I realized faith was never control. It was trust. Trust that the system still runs even when I don't touch the controls.

Anchor Card

Closed Loop Faith: *Grace operates as feedback, not broadcast.*

Principle: *Faith adjusts output based on response.*

Protocol: *Monitor emotion, recalibrate practice, repeat with humility.*

Proof: *Each honest audit reduced noise and increased stability.*

Observation logged

Chapter 13

God in the Data

Grace through calibration

Reading the Black Box

When an aircraft goes down, the first thing investigators look for is not the wreckage. It is the black box. Inside that small, nearly indestructible recorder are the final seconds before failure. Altitude, pressure, control inputs, and the crew's last words. The truth does not hide in the explosion. It hides in the numbers leading up to it. My life had been the same way. For years I could not stop staring at the wreckage. The bottles, the holes in the walls, the broken trust, the words I can never take back. I kept replaying the chaos, searching for meaning in the smoke. But after everything went silent, when the world finally stopped spinning, I realized I had been looking in the wrong place. The wreck was not where the answers lived. The truth was buried in the data. The choices, the habits, the micro decisions that stacked until the system failed. I started digging. Not emotionally, but literally. I opened my phone, my bank records, my text logs. I scrolled through photos and timestamps, mapping every night I drank to the hour. It was brutal, like performing an autopsy on my own soul. But the patterns were undeniable. The spiral was not random. The signals were there the whole time. Stress spikes before blackouts, fights after skipped meals, silence from Stacie whenever I had promised change and delivered chaos instead. Entropy had a rhythm. Pain had coordinates. Even grace had a pattern. It always arrived in the same places where I should have been destroyed but was not. That was when it hit me. God does not erase our black boxes. He teaches us to read them. Faith does not delete the crash. It decodes the message. Every scar, every sleepless night, every shattered plate held data. Not just tragedy but truth. And the more I studied it, the clearer it became. The systems that failed were never random. They revealed weak structures, faulty wiring, ignored warnings, pride where humility was supposed to go. The systems that held, the quiet love from my wife, the laughter from my son even when I did not deserve it, my brother showing up and driving across the country on a moments notice, those were proof of divine design. Every failure was a stress test. Every act of mercy was a calibration signal. Every unanswered prayer was a delay function built to align timing. Even silence was communication. A command that said, analyze, do not react. I had spent years asking why God was silent when He had been speaking in data the entire time. I just was not listening. The black box did not hold death. It held instructions. And for the first time in my life, I stopped feeling punished and started feeling studied. Not as an experiment, but as a system in need of tuning.

Feedback Equilibrium

Every living mechanism survives through correction, not control. In circuits it is called negative feedback, in conscience it is called mercy. Both reduce error by returning the signal to center without destroying the system that produced it. Judgment amplifies deviation, mercy damps it. The soul's stability depends not on perfection but on how quickly it responds to its own distortion. Grace is simply feedback interpreted without shame. That is how recovery begins, when a system learns to listen to its own correction without fear. There was a night I sat on my porch with printouts spread across the table. Screenshots, messages, receipts, pieces of wreckage. Kage came out, saw the papers, and asked, "Are you in trouble again?" I smiled, tired, hollow, honest. "No, buddy. I am figuring out how I got here." He nodded like he understood more than I thought. "You are reading the story, huh?" I paused, my throat tight. "Yeah, something like that." That moment, that quiet understanding between us, was another data point. The system still had life in it. The transmission was not lost. Numbers do not hate you. They help you tell the truth. And that truth was not about guilt. It was about grace hiding in plain sight, proof that even my failures carried coordinates back to God.

Law of Reference Frame

Perception creates the first fault line. Every system reads truth through its own vibration, so what looks like error from one frame may register as balance from another. Observation always bends reality by proximity, the closer you are to the signal, the more distortion you must correct for. Humility is the recalibration that realigns perspective to truth. Without it, interpretation becomes interference and feedback becomes judgment. Recovery begins when the observer adjusts, not when the system apologizes. You learn this the hard way. When chaos hits, the instinct is to zoom in and to fix, to dissect, to control. But the closer you get, the more the data shifts. A parent looking at a child sees rebellion, a teacher sees confusion, God sees design still forming. Each frame reads the same waveform differently. None of them are wrong. Some are just incomplete. The truth exists between them, at a point of parallax only humility can triangulate. In engineering, this is standard calibration. You never trust one sensor reading in isolation, you average across multiple sources until the deviation converges. In life, the process is the same. Grace is the averaging function. It doesn't erase the error, it absorbs it into proportion. Perspective, unchecked, becomes pride. Pride misreads alignment as threat. It filters everything through self-preservation and calls it clarity. That's how relationships fracture. Two observers mistaking their own reference frames for truth itself. Every argument is a data war between vantage points. But when one side stops demanding correction and starts adjusting its own coordinates, the signal clears. That's what humility really is. It is not weakness, not submission, but recalibration. It's the act of acknowledging that truth doesn't orbit you. It means stepping back far enough to see the curve you couldn't from inside the loop. From a new altitude, what looked like chaos often resolves into pattern. The heat map flattens. The noise resolves into design. Even God practices perspective. Omniscience doesn't mean He stares from one fixed position, it means He sees from all of them at once. That's why mercy exists. To bridge the gap between divine precision and human perception. Every fracture in communication, every loop of misunderstanding, every spiritual delay, all of it comes back to reference error. Observation without humility amplifies distortion. Observation with humility turns it into data. When you finally stop defending your angle and start aligning to truth itself, reality steadies. The vibration that once tore you apart becomes the hum that holds you together.

Grace as Calibration

For most of my life I thought grace meant forgiveness, a reset button for when I broke something again. But grace is not a pat on the head. It is calibration. When a system overheats, you add coolant. When it drifts off target, you adjust thrust. When pressure threatens to break structure, you reinforce it. Grace does all of that. It is

God's engineering intervention. When the sheriff let me go that night instead of arresting me, that was grace. When my brother drove hours to get me without a lecture, that was grace. Stacie being by my side for everything, that was grace. When my body somehow held on through years of abuse, that was grace. Grace did not always feel gentle. Sometimes it burned. Sometimes it hurt like being pulled through fire. Sometimes it came as silence, a heavy pause between prayers that felt unanswered. But every time, it corrected my trajectory. That was when I started seeing grace differently. It was not abstract or emotional. It was physics. Every correction, every delay, every consequence was calibration. Grace does not erase drift. It stabilizes it. It does not stop the shaking. It teaches you to read it. The hangovers were data. The shame was data. The small moments of peace were data. Grace used them all. I started praying differently too. Not for success or forgiveness, but for course correction. "God, correct me gently and quickly." That one line saved me more than any sermon ever did. Sometimes the correction came as exhaustion, forcing me to rest. Sometimes it came as conviction, forcing me to stop lying to myself. Sometimes it came as compassion, a stranger saying something kind when I least deserved it. All of it, calibration. I began logging my spiritual telemetry the way I used to log rocket data. Each night before bed, I noted what drifted, what held, what failed, what aligned. No self hatred. Just data. Over time I noticed the drift shrinking. The oscillations narrowed. My life, still imperfect and messy, began to stabilize. I was not swinging between extremes anymore. I was learning to fly within tolerance. Grace taught me that turbulence is not failure. It is feedback. You do not hate the shaking, you learn from it. Because if you are shaking, it means the system is still active. You are still connected to the source. The real danger is not turbulence. It is disconnection. I used to see grace as something I earned by repentance. Now I know it is the force that allows repentance to exist at all. Grace runs the system even when you have stopped believing in it. It keeps the current flowing long enough for you to find signal again. That is not softness. That is divine precision.

Anchor Card

Thermodynamic Paradox of Stillness: *Energy Without Motion*

Principle: *Stillness is not absence of power, it is contained potential.*

Protocol: *In thermodynamics, equilibrium holds maximum energy in perfect proportion, no loss, no waste. Spirit works the same way: when the soul stops striving, energy converts from combustion to coherence.*

Proof: *Rest is not the end of motion, it is motion mastered. Peace is the highest efficiency state, zero friction, full transmission.*

Observation logged

Signal Flare

For most of my life I was trying to prove something. That I could outwork pain, outthink addiction, outrun shame. I thought survival was validation, proof that I was in control. But I was not proving anything. I was just trying to send up a signal. To my parents. To my wife. To the world. To God. I wanted to be seen, heard, understood, loved. I kept firing flares into the dark, hoping someone would see the light. What I did not realize then was that the signal had been coming down the whole time. God had been transmitting since the beginning. I just was not tuned to the frequency. This story is my signal flare back. Not a trophy. Not a sermon. A flare from the pit for anyone still down there. A transmission that says you are not broken beyond repair. There is data in your pain. There is design in your survival. You are still alive, which means the system is not done running. When I finally started reading my own data through that lens, I saw how precise grace had been. The times I should have died but did not. The nights I should have been in jail but was not. The relationships I should have lost but somehow kept. Every near miss was a line of code that said you are still being guided. Entropy does not win by accident. It wins when you stop paying attention. But the moment you start reading your own black box, honestly, without editing or excuses, you begin to see it. God was never silent. We were just too loud. He had been broadcasting through every signal we called chaos. Through every heartbreak. Through every silence that was not abandonment, but bandwidth clearing for something better. One night I sat with Kage playing basketball out front. He asked, "Dad, do you ever think God talks through stuff that goes wrong?" I laughed a little, surprised. "That is the only way He has ever gotten through to me." He laughed and understood. "Then maybe some of the bad stuff that has happened was not just bad." My throat caught. "Maybe it was not." That was grace speaking through him, pure signal through a child's voice. So if you are holding your own black box, your mistakes, your guilt, your wreckage, do not erase it. Do not hide it. Read it. Log it. Decode it. There is truth inside that data. There is divine engineering inside your failure. The only difference between collapse and calibration is whether you pay attention. The system was never random. The chaos was never meaningless. And the design was never mine. Because all this time, the data did not just prove I survived. It proved I was guided. A few nights later I sat on the porch again. The air was cool and still, a low hum from the airport in the distance mixing with the faint chirp of crickets. Kage came out and sat beside me without a word. For a while we just watched the planes drift through the sky one by one, their lights blinking in perfect rhythm. He asked, "Do you ever think God talks through stuff like that?" I smiled. "I think He talks through everything that still moves." We sat there in silence, watching the planes cross the dark like measured pulses on a screen, and for the first time I felt no urge to fix or analyze anything. Just gratitude. The system was stable. The data made sense. The hum of the world felt like a heartbeat again, steady and alive. A field at equilibrium is never empty. Energy remains inside it, distributed so evenly that motion disappears. Stillness is not the death of force but its perfection. When every vector cancels its opposite, power hides inside peace. The body calls it rest. The spirit calls it surrender. The equation is the same. Total energy conserved, no heat wasted. What the world names silence is only balance measured correctly. And if you are still breathing, that means your telemetry is still transmitting. So read your black box, write one new line at the end, and execute the next correction in the next twenty four hours. That is how systems recover. That is how redemption runs. The crash was not your ending. It was your data collection. God is still running the analysis. The system still holds.

Anchor Card

Grace as Calibration: *Divine correction proves connection.*

Principle: *The system that still adjusts is alive.*

Protocol: *Welcome small disruptions, they prevent collapse.*

Proof: *Every course correction brought peace faster than pride ever did.*

Observation logged

Pattern detected

Epilogue

The Hidden Code of Reality

When the crash becomes creation and pattern is revealed

The Black Box Report

When I first started this investigation, I thought I was chasing an answer, something measurable, provable, a final theorem that could explain everything. I wanted to chart the coordinates of faith like a launch trajectory, plug in the data, find the pattern, confirm the truth. I did not realize I was already standing in it. What I found was not an equation. It was a pattern. Entropy was not just the law of decay. It was the law of exposure. When order breaks, truth bleeds through the cracks. The same rule that governs collapsing stars governs collapsing souls. When structure gives way, light escapes. The wreck does not hide the truth. It reveals it. That became the lens through which I saw everything. My failures, my relapses, my heartbreaks, my silence. The pain was not punishment. It was revelation. Every collapse was data, the divine diagnostic of a system designed to fail just enough to expose what needed repair. The more I studied it, the more I saw the geometry in the chaos. Every breakdown had symmetry. Every fracture had purpose. People spend their lives polishing the surface, patching the weak joints, painting over the rust. We pretend the system is stable because we are terrified of exposure. But God does not show Himself through perfection. He reveals Himself through fracture, through the seams where light leaks out. The clean data does not teach you, the corrupted data does. You do not find revelation in stability. You find it in the error logs. I had spent years thinking my life was a string of detours, addiction, failure, regret, as if I had wandered off the main road. But when I zoomed out far enough, I saw it differently. None of it was circular. It was spiral. Repeating, but never the same. Expanding and contracting in perfect proportion. The pattern was Fibonacci in spirit, a golden sequence of suffering and redemption curling endlessly toward order. Every time I broke, I was refining. Every time I fell, the arc widened. The same mathematical elegance that shapes galaxies was mirrored in my rebuilding. It was all there, the repeating ratio of chaos and grace, death and resurrection, entropy and order. The laws of physics mirrored in the laws of faith. Every equation balanced, even the ones that took decades to solve. Every mistake fed the next correction. Every loss refined the next act of mercy. Entropy pushed, grace pulled, and somehow, between the two, life held. One night I took Kage outside after a storm. The ground was soaked, the air heavy. We stood barefoot in the mud under the stars. He asked why the lightning looked like it was crawling across the sky. I told him, "That is energy looking for home." He nodded, eyes reflecting the flashes. "Like people." It stopped me cold. Out of the mouth of a child came the whole truth. We are all lightning trying to find ground. That was God, right there in the mud, speaking through my son, folding physics into mercy. I used to think faith was blind, that belief meant ignoring the evidence. But now I know faith is the highest form of observation. It is what happens when the data becomes undeniable but the meaning behind it still requires trust. It is not closing your eyes to the unknown. It is staring into it long enough to see the pattern forming through the static. I did not find God in sermons or rituals. I found Him in telemetry, in wreckage, in the faint hum that carried me through nights when I should have been dead. I found Him in every law I once used to disprove Him, in thermodynamics, in entropy, in gravity. Because the same laws that define the fall also define the lift. The system that allows chaos also guarantees calibration. The same energy that breaks you open is the one that rebuilds you stronger. If you are reading this, maybe you are standing in your own wreckage. Maybe your black box is full of static and guilt and questions you are afraid to ask. I know that feeling. The silence after the crash can sound like damnation. But I promise you it is not. The system is still running. The signal is still live. God is not gone. He is in the data. The fact that you are still breathing means the telemetry is still transmitting. You do not have to fix it all. You do not have to erase the crash. You just have to read it. Because hidden in every line of pain, in every fracture of faith, in every act of survival, there is a message. The code does not lie. It only hides until you are ready to see it. I spent most of my life chasing certainty, trying to prove that I was worth saving. Now I see that salvation is not earned. It is revealed. It is what happens when you stop trying to prove you are alive and start paying attention to the data that proves you already are. The universe is not silent. It speaks constantly, through equations, through scars, through grace disguised as coincidence. And the more you look, the more you see it. The ratio of redemption embedded in everything. The laws that govern rockets and galaxies and hearts all whisper the same truth. Nothing is wasted.

Final Transmission

The universe hums with equations we cannot fully write. The soul hums with pain we cannot fully name. And somewhere between them is the frequency of God, not shouting, not commanding, just whispering through the static, "You were never random. Every scar was part of the design." I did not just find order in the chaos. I found the Author in the algorithm. The voice behind the voltage. The mercy in the math. That is the hidden code of reality, the truth every system hints at, the message every survivor eventually decodes. The chaos was never the end. It was the proof of order waiting to be found. And the signal still runs. It always has. So if you are standing in the wreckage of your own life, do not erase it. Do not hide it. Read it. Decode it. There is order hiding in your disorder. There is purpose in your patterns. There is God in your data. That is the final truth of this book, the final revelation of my life. Entropy was not my enemy. It was the language God used to speak to me. The chaos was never punishment. It was communication. And the wreckage was not the end. It was the beginning of understanding. Outside, the rain started again, soft at first, then steady. The drops hit the trees and ground in rhythm, each one distinct but part of something larger, like code running through creation. The lights from the airport flickered through the mist, and for a moment the whole world seemed to breathe in sync. I sat there listening to the hum of it all and realized that peace was not stillness. It was movement without chaos. Every pulse, every sound, every second of it proof that the system was still running. God was still transmitting. The data was still alive.

Anchor Card

Final Transmission: *Failure leaves fingerprints of design.*

Principle: *Every end holds encoded beginnings.*

Protocol: *Review the crash not for guilt but for pattern.*

Proof: *Reading the data revealed the Designer's signature within every error log.*

Observation logged

Pattern detected

About the Author

Daniel Giavelli is a systems thinker whose work bridges the worlds of logic, faith, and human endurance. Before authoring this series, he spent years in high-intensity engineering environments, where precision and failure were constant teachers. His experiences on launch pads and in control rooms shaped the language of Against All Odds, a six-book exploration of collapse, calibration, and the quiet architecture of redemption. Daniel writes from lived experience rather than theory. His work blends the language of physics, psychology, and spirituality to reveal how design and grace follow the same laws. Each book in the series translates personal breakdowns into operating principles for recovery, faith, and resilience. He lives in South Texas, where he continues to build systems, both mechanical and human, that point toward proportion, truth, and renewal.

@AgainstAllOddsSeries

Against All Odds Vol.2 Coming Soon!

www.ingramcontent.com/pod-product-compliance
Lightning Source LLC
Chambersburg PA
CBHW060427130626
46555CB00005B/2242